Roald Dahl - Bernard Maclaverty
Graham Greene - Kate Chopin
Shirley Jackson

A World of Difference

Selected Short Stories by British and American Writers

by Gabriella Bonavoglia

First edition: April 1996

I owe special thanks to Margaret Cronin for her precious help and to my editors Rosalba Foreman and Elizabeth Holmes for their invaluable suggestions.

The publisher would like to thank the following for permission to reproduce copyright material: Murray Pollinger for "The Landlady" from *Kiss, Kiss* by Roald Dahl © 1959; Farrar, Straus & Giroux, Inc. for "The Lottery" from *The Lottery and Other Stories* by Shirley Jackson © 1948.

We would be happy to receive your comments and suggestions, and give you any other information concerning our material.

www.blackcat-cideb.com

ISBN 978-88-7754-268-7 Book + CD

Printed in Italy by Litoprint, Genoa

CONTENTS

PHONETIC SYMBOLS

Vowels

[ɪ]	*as in*	six
[i]	"	happy
[iː]	"	see
[e]	"	red
[æ]	"	hat
[ɑː]	"	car
[ɒ]	"	dog
[ɔː]	"	door
[ʊ]	"	put
[uː]	"	food
[ʌ]	"	cup
[ə]	"	about
[ɜː]	"	girl

Diphthongs

[eɪ]	*as in*	made
[aɪ]	"	five
[aʊ]	"	house
[ɔɪ]	"	boy
[əʊ]	"	home
[ɪə]	"	beer
[eə]	"	hair
[ʊə]	"	poor

Consonants

[b]	*as in*	bed
[k]	"	cat
[tʃ]	"	church
[d]	"	day
[f]	"	foot
[g]	"	good
[dʒ]	"	page
[h]	"	how
[j]	"	yes
[l]	"	leg
[m]	"	mum
[n]	"	nine
[ŋ]	"	sing
[p]	"	pen
[r]	"	red
[s]	"	soon
[z]	"	zoo
[ʃ]	"	show
[ʒ]	"	measure
[t]	"	tea
[θ]	"	thin
[ð]	"	this
[v]	"	voice
[w]	"	wine

[']   represents primary stress in the syllable which follows

[,]   represents secondary stress in the syllable which follows

[r]   indicates that the final "r" is only pronounced before a
word beginning with a vowel sound (British English).
In American English, the "r" is usually pronounced
before both consonants and vowel sounds.

INTRODUCTION

In writing this book we have made two basic assumptions. The first is that the short story is ideal way of introducing students to literature. Reading a complete text can give a genuine sense of satisfaction and, with a little initial guidance, short stories can be enjoyed by students reading on their own. In addition the great variety of themes and styles within the short story genre means that there is something to suit almost all tastes. The second assumption we have made is that the experienced reader has not merely stored facts about literature but has also been trained to respond to it.

The short stories in this volume have been selected according to their level of linguistic and thematic "difficulty". We have also tried to choose stories which students will find both accessible and stimulating.

Being able to make hypotheses and then check them against the text; to think about meaning and read between the lines; to compare ideas and concepts, and interpret texts are all skills acquired through guided interaction with the text. It is hoped that having acquired these skills, students will then be in a position to read on their own.

We have decided to divide some of the stories into shorter sections for several reasons:

- students may feel worried about confronting authentic texts for the first time;
- working with shorter extracts makes closer analysis easier;
- individual performance can be checked more frequently and students given as much guidance as necessary;
- lexical items or sentences for comment can be found more quickly.

We have included several different approaches to literary analysis:

- **Task-based**: a variety of activities which train the student to analyse texts and help them to become familiar with the methodology of literary analysis;
- **Step-by-step**: students 'uncover' the text in stages;
- **Cyclical**: information and understanding picked up at each stage is used again later, to be expanded and adjusted in the light of new information.

The activities can be divided into two types.

1 Comprehension activities helping students to understand language on two levels; both semantically, and at a deeper level, to read between the lines and infer meaning.

2 Analytical activities which provide the students with the tools to become competent in literary appreciation, familiarizing them with notions such as style, structure, theme and plot.

While some activities require a specific answer, others may be interpreted in several different ways, provided that answers are always backed up by examples or quotations from the text.

The book also includes:

- a glossary of literary terms, explaining terminology necessary for literary analysis;
- footnotes explaining more difficult words;
- culture reference boxes providing supplementary information about culture and geographical locations;
- follow-up activities in the section **BEYOND THE TEXT** practising writing skills, and using newspaper articles on subjects directly related to each story as a springboard for class discussion.

GLOSSARY OF LITERARY TERMS

Characterization: The way in which the personality and physical appearance of characters are presented in a piece of fiction.

Characters: The people that inhabit the fictional world.

Climax: The crucial part of a story, characterized by an increase of tension. The climax may be a crisis or a turning point for the main character.

Coherence: The way sentences combine in a text to produce meaning or "sense units".

Cohesion: The way sentences or part of them combine to form grammatical "units", for which purpose connectors, pronouns, substitutive verb forms etc. are used.

Connotation: Implications and associations that a word carries in addition to its literal meaning. Cf. **denotation**: The dictionary definition or literal meaning of a word.

End: When the initial situation in a story is overturned, maintained or re-established (conflict remains or is unresolved). By analysing how the story proceeds and by comparing its constituent parts (ie. the opening to the ending) we can draw conclusions about the structure of the story (linear, circular, spiral etc.).

Euphemism: A neutral expression or word used to replace either a concept or a word which is considered offensive or unpleasant; sometimes used for humorous effect.

Event: Something happens, a conflict starts, new characters may be introduced.

Figurative language: Language which uses figures of speech such as metaphors, similes, symbols, images etc., requiring imaginative interpretation.

Flashback: A literary device used to supply information about events which occurred before the beginning of the story.

Further development: The conflict continues, a climax is generally built up, another character may be introduced.

Graphological and paratextual features: Peculiarities in spacing, lay-out, use of italics or boldface etc.

Irony: Words and expressions used to suggest the opposite of what they mean. Irony may also result from a discrepancy between appearance and reality.

Metaphor: An imaginative comparison where one thing is described in terms of another. For example, "storm of grief" in "The Story of an Hour", (*l. 16*, page 112).

Modes: Report, description, dialogue and comment are all narrative modes.

Narrator: The narrator "tells" the story and may be either directly involved in the story, the first-person narrator, or external to the events being recounted, the third-person narrator.

A *first-person narrator* tells the story as a protagonist, or reports events s/he has witnessed. It is through his/her point of view that the reader has access to the fictional world, as such this narrative perspective is generally restricted and may be "unreliable".

The *third-person narrator* can be omniscient, non-omniscient or an external eye-witness. Writers may use a mixture of techniques, describing characters and events from shifting points of view.

The omniscient narrator knows everything about the characters.

The non-omniscient narrator tells the story from a limited perspective.

The external eye-witness reports only what can be seen from the outside and does not have access to the characters' thoughts.

The third-person narrator may be to varying degrees: intrusive, intervening in the narrative with comments and opinions or unintrusive, avoiding explicit comments.

Point of view: The position from which a story is told, or the perspective from which events are seen. It may be that of the narrator or any of the characters. The point of view may shift in a work of fiction.

Setting: The time and place where the events of a story take place.

Simile: A comparison drawn explicitly between two different things.

Story: The events of a narrative taken in chronological order.

Story pattern/plot: The arrangement of events in the narrative.

Style: How a particular writer says things: his choice of words, figures of speech (which include metaphor, simile, onomatopœia etc.), sentence structure.

Symbol: Generally, anything which stands for something else. It is often something concrete which is used to represent an abstract quality; for example a dove symbolizes peace, a rose, beauty.

Tone: Can be compared to tone of voice in speech and could be ironic, friendly, sympathetic, detached etc. It may be said to reflect the personality and outlook of the author.

"What is it to us whether these stories be true or false, so long as we can persuade ourselves into belief of them, and enjoy all the charm of the reality?"

Geoffrey Crayon

These symbols indicate the beginning and end of the four stories recorded on the cassette.

The Umbrella Man

by Roald Dahl

ROALD DAHL was born in South Wales in 1916 of Norwegian parents.

During the 2nd World War he served as an RAF pilot in Greece, Syria and Libya, where he was seriously wounded.

In 1942 he was posted to Washington as Assistant Air Attaché and his first short stories, mostly based on his wartime experiences, date back to that period.

There followed several collections of short stories which were highly acclaimed by critics and public alike and have been translated into many languages.

His publications include: *Someone Like You, Kiss Kiss, Switch Bitch, Ah, Sweet Mystery of Life, Tales of the Unexpected, Roald Dahl's Book of Ghost Stories*, and a novel *My Uncle Oswald*.

He also wrote many highly successful children's books including *Charlie and the Chocolate Factory, The Magic Finger, Fantastic Mr Fox, The Witches* and *Matilda*.

Roald Dahl is also remembered for inventing the Gremlins, which became popular all over the world after a film version of his book was made by Walt Disney.

He died in November 1990.

Before reading

1 How do you react if a stranger comes up to you? Do you agree with any of the statements given below? Give reasons for your choice(s).

- Always be suspicious of strangers.
- Do not judge people by appearances.
- Trust people and you will be rewarded.
- You can trust people if they are well-dressed and distinguished-looking.
- The nicer people seem to be, the less you should trust them!

2 Look at the title of the story. What do you expect the story to be about?
Tick one of the alternatives below:

- a man who repairs umbrellas
- a man who has found an umbrella
- a man who offers his umbrella to someone

3 Imagine you have gone out to do some shopping. The weather is fine at first but then it suddenly changes and it starts raining heavily. You do not have an umbrella with you. A man sheltering under a large umbrella comes up to you.
What would you expect him to say?

4 Listen to the first part of the story twice. Decide if the following statements are true or false and tick accordingly. Then read the text to check your results.

	True	False
a The story is set in Wales.	☐	☐
b The weather is bad.	☐	☐
c The "girl" narrator is 20 years old.	☐	☐
d She went to the dentist's.	☐	☐
e Her mother is with her.	☐	☐
f A tall, middle-aged man approaches them.	☐	☐

3

I'M GOING to tell you about a funny thing that happened to my mother and me yesterday evening. I am twelve years old and I'm a girl. My mother is thirty-four but I am nearly [1] as tall as her already. Yesterday afternoon, my mother took me up to London to see the dentist. He found one hole. It was in a back tooth and he filled it without hurting me too much. After that, we went to a café. I had a banana split [2] and my mother had a cup of coffee. By the time we got up to leave, it was about six o'clock.

When we came out of the café it had started to rain. 'We must get a taxi,' my mother said. We were wearing ordinary hats and coats, and it was raining quite hard.

'Why don't we go back into the café and wait for it to stop?' I said. I wanted another of those banana splits. They were gorgeous. [3]

'It isn't going to stop,' my mother said. 'We must get home.'

We stood on the pavement in the rain, looking for a taxi. Lots of them came by but they all had passengers inside them. 'I wish we had a car with a chauffeur,' my mother said.

Just then a man came up to us. He was a small man and he was pretty old, probably seventy or more. He raised his hat politely and said to my mother, 'Excuse me, I do hope you will excuse me ...' He had a fine white moustache and bushy [4] white eyebrows and a wrinkly [5] pink face. He was sheltering under an umbrella which he held high over his head.

'Yes?' my mother said, very cool and distant.

'I wonder if I could ask a small favour of you,' he said. 'It is only a very small favour.'

---

1 **nearly** : almost.
2 **banana split** : banana cut in half and served with ice-cream.
3 **gorgeous** ['gɔːdʒəs] : (here) delicious.
4 **bushy** ['buʃi] : thick with hair.
5 **wrinkly** ['rɪnkli] : with small folds or lines in the skin showing age.

5 What favour do you think the umbrella man will ask? Discuss in pairs.

6 Now listen to the next part of the story and then answer the questions on page 6.

I saw my mother looking at him suspiciously. She is a suspicious person, my mother. She is especially suspicious of two things – strange men and boiled eggs. When she cuts the top off a boiled egg, she pokes around inside it with her spoon as though expecting to find a mouse or something. With strange men, she has a golden rule which says, 'The   30
nicer the man seems to be, the more suspicious you must become.' This little old man was particularly nice. He was polite. He was well-spoken. He was well-dressed. He was a real gentleman. The reason I knew he was a gentleman was because of his shoes. 'You can always spot a gentleman by the shoes he wears,' was another of my mother's favourite sayings. [6]   35
This man had beautiful brown shoes.
   'The truth of the matter is,' the little man was saying, 'I've got myself into a bit of a scrape. [7] I need some help. Not much I assure you. It's almost nothing, in fact, but I do need it. You see, madam, old people like me often become terribly forgetful ...'   40
   My mother's chin was up and she was staring down at him along the full length of her nose. It was a fearsome [8] thing, this frosty-nosed stare [9] of my mother's. Most people go to pieces completely when she gives it to them. I once saw my own headmistress begin to stammer [10] and simper like an idiot when my mother gave her a really foul [11] frosty-noser. But   45

---

6   **sayings** : (here) often repeated expressions.

7   **scrape** [skreɪp] : (infml) embarassing situation.

8   **fearsome** [ˈfɪəsəm] : frightening.

9   **frosty-nosed stare** : cold look of superiority and hostility.

10   **stammer** : speak with rapid repetitions of same syllable.

11   **foul** [faʊl] : terrible.

the little man on the pavement with the umbrella over his head didn't bat an eyelid. He gave a gentle smile and said, 'I beg you to believe, madam, that I am not in the habit of stopping ladies in the street and telling them my troubles.'

50 'I should hope not,' my mother said.

I felt quite embarrassed by my mother's sharpness. I wanted to say to her, 'Oh, mummy, for heaven's sake, he's a very very old man, and he's sweet and polite, and he's in some sort of trouble, so don't be so beastly 12 to him.' But I didn't say anything.

55 The little man shifted his umbrella from one hand to the other. 'I've never forgotten it before,' he said.

'You've never forgotten what?' my mother asked sternly. 13

'My wallet,' he said. 'I must have left it in my other jacket. Isn't that the silliest thing to do?'

60 'Are you asking me to give you money?' my mother said.

'Oh, good gracious me, 14 no!' he cried. 'Heaven forbid I should ever do that!'

'Then what are you asking?' my mother said. 'Do hurry up. We're getting soaked to the skin 15 here.'

65 'I know you are,' he said. 'And that is why I'm offering you this umbrella of mine to protect you, and to keep forever, if ... if only ...'

'If only what?' my mother said.

'If only you would give me in return a pound for my taxi-fare 16 just to get me home.'

a What favour did the umbrella man ask?
b What reason did he give for having to ask this favour?

Were your predictions right?

12 **beastly** ['biːstli] : unpleasant, unkind.
13 **sternly** [stɜːnli] : seriously, disapprovingly.
14 **good gracious me** : (dated) exclamation of surprise or indignation.
15 **soaked to the skin** : (idm) completely wet.
16 **taxi-fare** ['tæksi feə] : money charged for a journey by taxi.

7 Find these phrases in the text, then look at how they are used in context, read the definitions given and tick the one you think is right.

a pokes around inside it:
- ☐ mixes it around very quickly
- ☐ makes little pushing movements, showing suspicion
- ☐ doesn't concentrate on what she is doing

b staring down:
- ☐ looking at someone kindly, showing sympathy
- ☐ looking at someone with indifference
- ☐ looking at someone in a condescending way

c go to pieces:
- ☐ feel a little uneasy but soon recover
- ☐ lose control of themselves because they are upset or nervous
- ☐ can't speak

d didn't bat an eyelid:
- ☐ didn't react
- ☐ didn't move his eyes
- ☐ was impatient

8 Look back at Extracts 1 and 2. Fill in the table below with information about the characters introduced by the "girl" narrator.

	MAN	MOTHER
Physical details		
Psychological details		

Which character does the "girl" narrator sympathize with most?

9 Look at two of the mother's sayings.

- "The nicer the man seems to be, the more suspicious you must become."
- "You can always spot a gentleman by the shoes he wears."

What is strange about them?

10 Go through the list of adjectives below and in the spaces provided write the one(s) you consider appropriate to each character (if you are not sure read on before deciding).

- trustworthy
- inconsistent
- short-tempered
- conceited
- well-mannered

- sensitive
- prejudiced
- generous
- wise
- polite

- witty
- snobbish
- unfriendly
- critical
- rude

- independent
- pompous
- persistent
- authoritarian
- eccentric

GIRL	
HER MOTHER	
THE MAN	

11 Complete the outline below to obtain a short summary of the story so far.

A mother had taken her _____

Once out in the street it _____ hard. They didn't

have an _____ suggested they

should get a taxi back home. Just then a man _____

He asked _____: as he _____

and he had no money on him he would be glad to exchange his _____

_____

12 How do you expect the woman to react? Tick your choice.

- She will immediately accept: it seems a real bargain!
- She will take some time to make up her mind but she eventually accepts.
- She definitely doesn't want to take the umbrella: the man is a trickster.

13 Read the next section and then answer the questions on page 11.

My mother was still suspicious. 'If you had no money in the first   70
place,' she said, 'then how did you get here?'

'I walked,' he answered. 'Every day I go for a lovely long walk and
then I summon [17] a taxi to take me home. I do it every day of the year.'

Why don't you walk home now?' my mother asked.

'Oh, I wish I could,' he said. 'I do wish I could. But I don't think I   75
could manage it on these silly old legs of mine. I've gone too far already.'

My mother stood there chewing her lower lip. She was beginning to
melt a bit, [18] I could see that. And the idea of getting an umbrella to

17   **summon** ['sʌmən] : (fml) (here) call.
18   **melt a bit** : soften a little.

shelter under must have tempted her a good deal.

80 'It's a lovely umbrella,' the little man said.

'So I've noticed,' my mother said.

'It's silk,' he said.

'I can see that.'

'Then why don't you take it, madam,' he said. 'It cost me over twenty
85 pounds, I promise you. But that's of no importance so long as I can get
home and rest these old legs of mine.'

I saw my mother's hand feeling for [19] the clasp [20] of her purse. She saw
me watching her. I was giving her one of my *own* frosty-nosed looks this
time and she knew exactly what I was telling her. Now listen, mummy, I
90 was telling her, you simply *mustn't* take advantage of a tired old man in
this way. It's a rotten [21] thing to do. My mother paused and looked back
at me. Then she said to the little man, 'I don't think it's quite right that I
should take an umbrella from you worth twenty pounds. I think I'd
better just *give* you the taxi-fare and be done with it.'

95 'No, no no!' he cried. 'It's out of the question! I wouldn't dream of it!
Not in a million years! I would never accept money from you like that!
Take the umbrella, dear lady, and keep the rain off your shoulders!' [22]

My mother gave me a triumphant sideways [23] look. There you are, she
was telling me. You're wrong. He *wants* me to have it.

100 She fished into [24] her purse and took out a pound note. She held it out
to the little man. He took it and handed her the umbrella. He pocketed
the pound, raised his hat, gave a quick bow [25] from the waist, [26] and said,
'Thank you, madam, thank you.' Then he was gone.

'Come under here and keep dry, darling,' my mother said. 'Aren't we
105 lucky. I've never had a silk umbrella before. I couldn't afford it.'

---

19   **feeling for** : trying to find.

20   **clasp** : metal fastening to open / close a bag.

21   **rotten** ['rɒtn] : (infml) terrible.

22   **keep the rain off your shoulders** : protect yourself from the rain.

23   **sideways** : from one side.

24   **fished into** : searched for something inside.

25   **bow** [baʊ] : bending forward as a sign of respect.

26   **waist** [weɪst] : part of the body where trousers and skirts are belted.

Why were you so horrid [27] to him in the beginning?' I asked.

I wanted to satisfy myself he wasn't a trickster,' [28] she said. 'And I did. He was a gentleman. I'm very pleased I was able to help him.'

'Yes, mummy,' I said.

'A *real* gentleman,' she went on. 'Wealthy, too, otherwise he wouldn't   110 have had a silk umbrella. I shouldn't be surprised if he isn't a titled person. Sir Harry Goldsworthy or something like that.'

'Yes, mummy.'

'This will be a good lesson to you,' she went on. 'Never rush things. Always take your time when you are summing someone up. [29] Then   115 you'll never make mistakes.'

a What does the woman think of the man now?
b What arguments does she use to support her opinion?

Were your predictions right?

14 Think about how the story could develop. Select one of the alternatives given below:

- the man will disappear and the girl's mother will realize she has been robbed;
- the man will come back soon afterwards with a new request;
- the man will reappear saying he no longer needs the pound note and wants his umbrella back;
- the man won't call a taxi but will go down a side street and make for a pub.

15 Listen to the next part of the story to check your predictions.

---

27   **horrid** ['hɒrɪd] : rude.

28   **trickster** : person who deceives by tricking or cheating other people.

29   **summing someone up** : forming an opinion of someone.

'There he goes,' I said. 'Look.'

'Where?'

'Over there. He's crossing the street. Goodness, mummy, what a hurry
120 he's in.'

We watched the little man as he dodged nimbly [30] in and out of the
traffic. When he reached the other side of the street, he turned left,
walking very fast.

'He doesn't look very tired to me, does he to you, mummy?'
125 My mother didn't answer.

'He doesn't look as though he's trying to get a taxi, either,' I said.

My mother was standing very still and stiff, [31] staring across the street
at the little man. We could see him clearly. He was in a terrific [32] hurry.
He was bustling [33] along the pavement, sidestepping [34] the other
130 pedestrians [35] and swinging [36] his arms like a soldier on the march.

'He's up to something,' my mother said, stony-faced.

'But what?'

'I don't know,' my mother snapped. [37] 'But I'm going to find out.
Come with me.' She took my arm and we crossed the street together.
135 Then we turned left.

'Can you see him?' my mother asked.

'Yes. There he is. He's turning right down the next street.'

We came to the corner and turned right. The little man was about
twenty yards ahead of us. He was scuttling along [38] like a rabbit and we
140 had to walk very fast to keep up with him. The rain was pelting down [39]

---

30   **dodged nimbly** : moved quickly and with agility.

31   **stiff** : rigidly.

32   **terrific** : (infml) great.

33   **bustling** ['bʌstlɪŋ] : moving in a hurried and busy way.

34   **sidestepping** : stepping to one side to avoid contact.

35   **pedestrians** [pə'destrɪən] : people walking on the pavement.

36   **swinging** : (here) moving backwards and forwards.

37   **snapped** : said irritably.

38   **scuttling** ['skʌtlɪŋ] **along** : running with quick steps.

39   **pelting down** : falling heavily and continuously.

harder than ever now and I could see it dripping from the brim [40] of his hat on to his shoulders. But we were snug [41] and dry under our lovely big silk umbrella.

'What is he up to?' my mother said.

'What if he turns round and sees us?' I asked. 145

'I don't care if he does,' my mother said. 'He lied to us. He said he was too tired to walk any further and he's practically running us off our feet! [42] He's a barefaced liar! [43] He's a crook!' [44]

'You mean he's *not* a titled gentleman?' I asked.

'Be quiet,' she said. 150

At the next crossing, the little man turned right again.

Then he turned left.

Then right.

'I'm not giving up now,' my mother said.

'He's disappeared!' I cried. Where's he gone?' 155

'He went in that door!' my mother said. 'I saw him! Into that house! Great heavens, it's a pub!'

16 Now focus on the man's behaviour and the woman's attitude towards him. Scan the text and make notes on what he does and how she reacts. Some examples are given in the table on the next page. Has this part of the story added anything to your knowledge of the characters, or has it simply confirmed your previous impressions?

---

40 **brim** : edge (of a hat).

41 **snug** [snʌg] : sheltered and comfortable.

42 **running us off our feet** : making us run so fast that it is difficult to keep up with him.

43 **barefaced liar** : person who tells lies shamelessly.

44 **crook** [krʊk] : (infml) dishonest person, professional criminal.

MAN'S ACTIONS	WOMAN'S REACTIONS

He crosses the street...
reaches the other
side... walking very fast

She stands still and stiff

He is in a terrific hurry ....
....
....
....
....

She is ....
....

He turns right down ....
....
....
....

She now considers him a ....
....
....

He enters a pub

She is astonished

17 Read the last part of the story and say if the following statements are true or false, then correct the false ones.

		True	False
a	The mother and her daughter went into the pub.	☐	☐
b	It had stopped raining.	☐	☐
c	The pub was crowded but no one was smoking.	☐	☐
d	The man had a double whisky which he drank very slowly.	☐	☐
e	Before going out he took one of the many wet umbrellas by the door of the pub.	☐	☐
f	He took it in a very ostentatious way.	☐	☐
g	Neither the mother nor the daughter could understand what he was trying to do.	☐	☐
h	The man stopped a person to offer him his new umbrella.	☐	☐

It was a pub. In big letters right across the front it said THE RED LION.
'You're not going in are you, mummy?'
160 'No,' she said. We'll watch from outside.'
There was a big plate-glass [45] window along the front of the pub, and
although it was a bit steamy [46] on the inside, we could see through it very
well if we went close.
We stood huddled [47] together outside the pub window. I was
165 clutching my mother's arm. The big raindrops were making a loud noise
on our umbrella. 'There he is,' I said. 'Over there.'
The room we were looking into was full of people and cigarette
smoke, and our little man was in the middle of it all. He was now without
his hat and coat, and he was edging his way [48] through the crowd
170 towards the bar. When he reached it, he placed both hands on the bar
itself and spoke to the barman. I saw his lips moving as he gave his order.
The barman turned away from him for a few seconds and came back with
a smallish tumbler [49] filled to the brim [50] with light brown liquid. The
little man placed a pound note on the counter.
175 'That's my pound!' my mother hissed. 'By golly, [51] he's got a nerve!' [52]
What's in the glass?' I asked.
'Whisky,' my mother said. 'Neat whisky.'
The barman didn't give him any change from the pound.
'That must be a treble whisky,' my mummy said.
180 'What's a treble?' I asked.
'Three times the normal measure,' she answered.
The little man picked up the glass and put it to his lips. He tilted [53] it
gently. Then he tilted it higher ... and higher ... and higher ... and very

---

45 **plate-glass** : fine quality glass for shop windows.
46 **steamy** ['sti:mi] : full of vapour.
47 **huddled** : close.
48 **edging his way** : move slowly and carefully.
49 **tumbler** ['tʌmblə] : glass for drinking spirits.
50 **brim** : the top of the glass.
51 **by golly** : (dated, infml) expression of surprise.
52 **he's got a nerve** : what impudence.
53 **tilted** : raised (in a sloping position).

soon all the whisky had disappeared down his throat in one long pour. [54]

'That's a jolly [55] expensive drink,' I said. 185

'It's ridiculous!' my mummy said. 'Fancy paying a pound for something to swallow [56] in one go!'

'It cost him more than a pound,' I said. 'It cost him a twenty-pound silk umbrella.'

'So it did,' my mother said. 'He must be mad.' 190

The little man was standing by the bar with the empty glass in his hand. He was smiling now, and a sort of golden glow [57] of pleasure was spreading over his round pink face. I saw his tongue come out to lick the white moustache, as though searching for one last drop of that precious whisky. 195

Slowly, he turned away from the bar and edged his way back [58] through the crowd to where his hat and coat were hanging. He put on his hat. He put on his coat. Then, in a manner so superbly cool and casual that you hardly noticed anything at all, he lifted from the coatrack one of the many wet umbrellas hanging there, and off he went. 200

'Did you see that!' my mother shrieked. 'Did you see what he did!

'Ssshh!' I whispered. 'He's coming out!'

We lowered our umbrella to hide our faces, and peeped out [59] from under it.

Out he came. But he never looked in our direction. He opened his new 205 umbrella over his head and scurried [60] off down the road the way he had come.

'So that's his little game!' my mother said.

'Neat,' I said. 'Super.'

We followed him back to the main street where we had first met him, 210 and we watched him as he proceeded, with no trouble at all, to exchange

54 **pour** : drink.

55 **jolly** : (infml) very.

56 **swallow** ['swɒləʊ] : pass down your throat.

57 **glow** [gləʊ] : warm look.

58 **edged ... back** : moved carefully back (to the door).

59 **peeped out** ['piːpt 'aʊt] : looked quickly and secretively.

60 **scurried** ['skʌrɪd] : ran hurriedly with short, quick steps.

his new umbrella for another pound note. This time it was with a tall thin fellow [61] who didn't even have a coat or hat. And as soon as the transaction [62] was completed, our little man trotted [63] off down the street

215 and was lost in the crowd. But this time he went in the opposite direction.

'You see how clever he is!' my mother said. 'He never goes to the same pub twice!'

'He could go on doing this all night,' I said.

'Yes,' my mother said. 'Of course. But I'll bet he prays like mad for

220 rainy days.'

18 Go back to Activity 10 and think about the characters again. Has your opinion of them been confirmed or has it changed? Add more adjectives to the table or change them if necessary.

Now reconsider the story as a whole.

19 Look back at the story, does it have an introduction, a climax and a conclusion? Underline the parts of the story accordingly.

Look at the episodes at the beginning of the story (when the man stops the mother and daughter), and the conclusion. Is the initial situation overturned or re-established? What is the structure of the story?

20 There are many ways to organize the material in a work of fiction. For example certain information can be revealed at a later stage to increase interest, expectation, suspense etc. List the main events of "The Umbrella Man" and decide if they proceed in chronological order. What effect does this particular structure produce?

---

61   **fellow** : (dated, infml) man.
62   **transaction** [trænz'ækʃən] : (here) business.
63   **trotted** : walked quickly (with small steps).

21 How does the author succeed in conveying a change in the man's behaviour in the central part of the story (*ll. 119-57*). Think about the following:

a The use of verbs – are they dynamic or static?

b The use of simile – what do they add to meaning?

c The lay-out in the lines given below:

"... the little man turned right again.
Then he turned left.
Then right."

What impression do such devices convey of the man?

22 Analysing the writer's style involves examining the language he uses: his choice of words, particular grammatical features, devices employed, register. Go through the list of possibilities given below and tick the ones you consider examples of informal style. Then refer back to this short story and draw your conclusions about its style.

- short sentences
- active voice
- imperative mood
- ungrammatical forms
- latinate words
- contracted forms

- complex subordinate sentences
- familiar words
- slang expressions
- emphatic inversions
- elliptical forms
- phrasal verbs

23 a In addition to an informal register, there is also a more formal register, characterized by more elaborate constructions and erudite language. Who uses this register?

- the woman
- the man
- the girl
- the "girl" narrator

Support your choice with examples from the text.

b Is there a discrepancy between the language you would expect from a twelve-year-old girl and the language actually used by the "girl" narrator? Find examples in the text to support your choice.

24 a This short story is recounted in the first person. How would you define the "girl" narrator?

- protagonist
- co-protagonist
- witness
- commentator
- other

b What are the advantages of using a first-person narrator? Look at the list below for suggestions and tick your choice with reference to the story you have just read.

- it makes the reader share the characters' emotions
- it makes the reader more involved in the story
- it arouses the reader's sympathy
- it gives credibility to the story
- it helps to build up suspense as the reader only knows what the character knows
- it gives the story a confidential tone

Are there any disadvantages?

25 Which of the following definitions could apply to the story?

- a surprise-ending story
- a close-ended story
- a humorous story
- a story with a moral
- a story based on incidents
- an anecdote

Beyond the text

Activity 1

Tell the story from the mother's viewpoint – imagine that she is reporting the episode to a friend of hers.

Activity 2

STEP 1

Discuss how the story could be adapted for dramatization. What problems might you have to solve?

- Look closely at the dialogue.
- Look at the descriptive and narrative passages. What information do they give you? Could they easily be adapted as "stage directions"? Which of the following features would you include in your stage directions?
  - description of the setting
  - description of characters
  - indications about tone of voice, facial expressions, movements, sound effects, etc.
  - background information
- Think about the setting.

  How would you deal with it?

  Do you think you could have problems changing scenes? If so, how would you overcome them?

  Is there any scene that you would give particular prominence to?

STEP 2

Work in groups and re-write the story (or part of it) as a play.
Divide it into scenes and use "stage directions".

Talking points

1 Young teenagers are easily influenced by the adult world, taking on the sayings, attitudes and gestures of the people around them. Do you agree? Give your reasons.

2 Read the article about the conman given below where, once again women are tricked. What exactly happens to Ms Wakelin? And to the old woman in the Skoda?

Conman [1] takes two women for a ride

BY JOE JOSEPH

AS STINGS [2] go, it was hardly in the Paul Newman-Robert Redford class.

A man driving a battered [3] orange Skoda travelled to the Wiltshire home of Patricia Wakelin, who had advertised her Y-registration Ford Fiesta for sale in a magazine called *Trade It*, having established it would be all right to take his aged granny along.

When he arrived in Westbury on Monday night, the Skoda's back seat was indeed occupied by an old woman. After giving the Fiesta the once over, kicking the tyres a few times, the smooth-tongued conman asked Ms Wakelin if he could take it for a test drive. Naturally he would leave the Skoda, with his granny in the back seat, as "security and collateral". [4]

When the man failed to return, and Ms Wakelin could not get any sense out of his "granny", she feared the worst and called the police.

Officers checked the Skoda's pedigree and found that it had been stolen from Fishponds, Bristol.

Sergeant David Thorn of Westbury Police said the old woman was clearly confused by everything. "She thought she was just being taken out for a drive in the country. It turned out she was from a home to which she has now returned. But it doesn't help us with the car."

(from THE TIMES)

1 **Conman** : Trickster.
2 **stings** : (Am. slang) cheats, swindles (here the word refers to the famous film of the same name).
3 **battered** ['bætəd] : old, damaged.
4 **security and collateral** : guarantee.

THE LANDLADY

by ROALD DAHL

The Landlady

Before reading

1 Look at the following definition of the word *landlady*: "a woman who owns and runs a small hotel". (*Longman Dictionary of Contemporary English*)

Now look at the words below all taken from the text. How would you link them to the title? Think of a possible story using the words below. Use any additional words you require.

- Billy Weaver
- Bath
- cheap hotel
- bed & breakfast

2 Read the beginning of the story and fill in the table on pages 26-7.

B ILLY WEAVER had travelled down from London on the slow afternoon train, with a change at Swindon on the way, and by the time he got to Bath it was about nine o'clock in the evening and the moon was coming up out of a clear starry [1] sky over the houses opposite the station entrance. But the air was 5
deadly cold and the wind was like a flat blade [2] of ice on his cheeks.

'Excuse me,' he said, 'but is there a fairly cheap hotel not too far away from here?'

'Try The Bell and Dragon,' the porter [3] answered, pointing down the road. 'They might take you in. It's about a quarter of a mile along on the 10
other side.'

---

1 **starry** ['stɑːri] : full of stars.
2 **blade** [bleɪd] : cutting part of a knife.
3 **porter** ['pɔːtə] : person who carries people's luggage in railways stations, airports, hotels etc.

Billy thanked him and picked up his suitcase and set out [4] to walk the quarter-mile to The Bell and Dragon. He had never been to Bath before. He didn't know anyone who lived there. But Mr Greenslade at the Head Office in London had told him it was a splendid city. 'Find your own lodgings,' [5] he had said, 'and then go along and report to the Branch [6] Manager as soon as you've got yourself settled.'

Billy was seventeen years old. He was wearing a new navy-blue overcoat, a new brown trilby hat, [7] and a new brown suit, and he was feeling fine. He walked briskly [8] down the street. He was trying to do everything briskly these days. Briskness, he had decided, was the one common characteristic of all successful businessmen. The big shots [9] up at Head Office were absolutely fantastically brisk [10] all the time. They were amazing. [11]

15

20

Culture reference

Bath	today a fashionable town in Avon, famous for its Roman baths, from which it takes its name

SETTING	**Place**	
	Time of the day	
	Weather	

4   **set out** : started.

5   **lodgings** ['lɒdʒɪŋz] : accommodation.

6   **Branch**: local office of a large company.

7   **trilby hat** : a man's soft hat made of felt.

8   **briskly** : quickly.

9   **shots** : (infml) important managers.

10   **brisk** : (here) active, full of energy.

11   **amazing** [ə'meɪzɪŋ] : incredible.

BILLY WEAVER	Age	
	Appearance	
	How he feels	
	....	
	Reason for his journey	
	....	

Read the next section and then do Activities **a** and **b** on page 29.

There were no shops in this wide street that he was walking along,   25
only a line of tall houses on each side, all of them identical. They had
porches and pillars 12 and four or five steps going up to their front doors,
and it was obvious that once upon a time they had been very swanky 13
residences. But now, even in the darkness, he could see that the paint
was peeling from the woodwork 14 on their doors and windows, and that   30
the handsome white façades were cracked 15 and blotchy 16 from neglect.

Suddenly, in a downstairs window that was brilliantly illuminated by
a street-lamp not six yards away, Billy caught sight of a printed notice
propped up 17 against the glass in one of the upper panes. 18 It said BED
AND BREAKFAST. There was a vase of pussy-willows, 19 tall and beautiful,   35
standing just underneath the notice.

He stopped walking. He moved a bit closer. Green curtains (some sort
of velvety material) were hanging down on either side of the window.

12   **pillars** ['pɪləz] : columns of stone.
13   **swanky** : fashionable and ostentatious.
14   **woodwork** ['wʊdwɜːk] : the wooden part.
15   **cracked** : damaged, broken.
16   **blotchy** ['blɒtʃi] : marked.
17   **propped up** : placed.
18   **panes** [peɪnz] : panels (of glass).
19   **pussy-willows** : soft, furry flowers of the willow tree.

The pussy-willows looked wonderful beside them. He went right up and
peered [20] through the glass into the room, and the first thing he saw was a
bright fire burning in the hearth. [21] On the carpet in front of the fire, a
pretty little dachshund [22] was curled up asleep with its nose tucked into [23]
its belly. The room itself, so far as he could see in the half-darkness, was
filled with pleasant furniture. There was a baby-grand piano [24] and a big
sofa and several plump armchairs; and in one corner he spotted a large
parrot in a cage. Animals were usually a good sign in a place like this,
Billy told himself; and all in all, it looked to him as though it would be a
pretty decent house to stay in. Certainly it would be more comfortable
than The Bell and Dragon.

On the other hand, a pub would be more congenial than a boarding-
house. There would be beer and darts [25] in the evenings, and lots of
people to talk to, and it would probably be a good bit cheaper, too. He
had stayed a couple of nights in a pub once before and he had liked it. He
had never stayed in any boarding-houses, and, to be perfectly honest, he
was a tiny [26] bit frightened of them. The name itself conjured up [27] images
of watery cabbage, rapacious [28] landladies, and a powerful smell of
kippers [29] in the living-room.

20 **peered** ['pɪəd] : looked closely.
21 **hearth** [hɑːθ] : fireplace.
22 **dachshund** ['dækshund] : type of small dog with long body and short legs.
23 **tucked into** : pressed against.
24 **baby-grand piano** : smaller version of a grand piano.
25 **darts** : (here) game in which pointed arrows are thrown (very common in English pubs).
26 **tiny** ['taini] : (here) little.
27 **conjured** ['kʌndʒəd] '**up** : evoked, suggested.
28 **rapacious** [rə'peɪʃəs] : greedy (esp. for money).
29 **kippers** : salted, smoked herrings.

a Focus on the descriptions of the street and the room. Fill in the table below with words and expressions from the text. Are the descriptions positive or negative? What is Billy's impression of his surroundings?

DESCRIPTION OF THE STREET	DESCRIPTION OF THE ROOM
....	....
....	....
....	....
....	....
....	....

b Explain why Billy doesn't go into the boarding-house immediately but thinks about other solutions before making his mind up.

4 What do you think Billy will do next?
- He will decide to stay at The Bell and Dragon.
- He will decide to stay at the boarding-house and will ring the bell.

5 Read the next part of the story and then fill in the table on page 32.

After dithering about [30] like this in the cold for two or three minutes, Billy decided that he would walk on and take a look at The Bell and Dragon before making up his mind. He turned to go.   60

And now a queer [31] thing happened to him. He was in the act of stepping back and turning away from the window when all at once his eye was caught and held in the most peculiar manner by the small notice that was there. BED AND BREAKFAST, it said. BED AND BREAKFAST, BED AND BREAKFAST, BED AND BREAKFAST. Each word was like a large black eye staring   65

---

30   dithering ['dɪðərɪŋ] about : (infml) hesitating.

31   queer : curious, odd.

at him through the glass, holding him, compelling him, forcing him to stay where he was and not to walk away from that house, and the next thing he knew, he was actually moving across from the window to the front door of the house, climbing the steps that led up to it, and reaching for the bell.

70   He pressed the bell. Far away in a back room he heard it ringing, and then *at once* – it must have been at once because he hadn't even had time to take his finger from the bell-button – the door swung open and a woman was standing there.

Normally you ring the bell and you have at least a half-minute's wait
75   before the door opens. But this dame was like a jack-in-the-box. [32] He pressed the bell - and out she popped! [33] It made him jump.

She was about forty-five or fifty years old, and the moment she saw him, she gave him a warm welcoming smile.

'*Please* come in,' she said pleasantly. She stepped aside, holding the
80   door wide open, and Billy found himself automatically starting forward into the house. The compulsion or, more accurately, the desire to follow after her into that house was extraordinarily strong.

'I saw the notice in the window,' he said, holding himself back.

'Yes, I know.'

85   'I was wondering about a room.'

'It's *all* ready for you, my dear,' she said. She had a round pink face and very gentle blue eyes.

'I was on my way to The Bell and Dragon,' Billy told her. 'But the notice in your window just happened to catch my eye.'

90   'My dear boy,' she said, 'why don't you come in out of the cold?'

'How much do you charge?' [34]

'Five and sixpence a night, including breakfast.'

It was fantastically cheap. It was less than half of what he had been willing to pay.

---

32   **jack-in-the-box** : a toy box with a puppet inside that springs up when the top is opened.

33   **popped** : appeared suddenly.

34   **How much ... charge?** : How much does it cost?

'If that is too much,' she added, 'then perhaps I can reduce it just a   95
tiny bit. Do you desire an egg for breakfast? Eggs are expensive at the
moment. It would be sixpence less without the egg.'

'Five and sixpence is fine,' he answered. 'I should like very much to
stay here.'

'I knew you would. Do come in.'   100

She seemed terribly nice. She looked exactly like the mother of one's
best school-friend welcoming one into the house to stay for the Christmas
holidays. Billy took off his hat, and stepped over the threshold. 35

'Just hang it there,' she said, 'and let me help you with your coat.'

There were no other hats or coats in the hall. There were no umbrellas,   105
no walking-sticks – nothing.

We have it *all* to ourselves,' she said, smiling at him over her shoulder
as she led the way upstairs. 'You see, it isn't very often I have the
pleasure of taking a visitor into my little nest.'

The old girl is slightly dotty, 36 Billy told himself. But at five and   110
sixpence a night, who gives a damn about that? 37 'I should've thought
you'd be simply swamped 38 with applicants,' 39 he said politely.

'Oh, I am, my dear, I am, of course I am. But the trouble is that I'm
inclined to be just a teeny weeny 40 bit choosey 41 and particular – if you
see what I mean.'   115

'Ah, yes.'

'But I'm always ready. Everything is always ready day and night in
this house just on the off-chance 42 that an acceptable 43 young gentleman
will come along. And it is such a pleasure, my dear, such a very great
pleasure when now and again I open the door and I see someone   120

---

35   **threshold** ['θreʃhəʊld] : entrance (of a house).

36   **dotty** : (infml) mad, eccentric.

37   **who gives a damn about that?** : (infml) who cares about that?

38   **swamped** [swɒmpt] : inundated.

39   **applicants** : (here) people looking for accommodation.

40   **a teeny weeny** ['tiːni'wiːni] : (infml) a little.

41   **choosey** ['tʃuːzi] : not easy to please.

42   **on the off-chance** : in case.

43   **acceptable** [ək'septəbl] : adequate.

standing there who is just *exactly* right.' She was half-way up the stairs, and she paused with one hand on the stair-rail, turning her head and smiling down at him with pale lips. 'Like you,' she added, and her blue eyes travelled slowly all the way down the length of Billy's body, to his feet, and then up again.

125

BILLY	The effect the notice had on him ....
THE LANDLADY	Age .... Appearance .... Behaviour ....

6 How do you expect the story to go on? Decide which of the alternatives below you agree with or think of your own suggestion.

- The landlady has a definite plan: she wants to seduce Billy.
- The landlady has a definite plan: she wants to steal his money.
- The landlady doesn't have any particular plan: she is just a little crazy.

7 Read the next section and say if Billy's first impression of the woman and the place is confirmed or not. Give evidence from the text to support your answer.

On the first-floor landing she said to him, 'This floor is mine.'

They climbed up a second flight. 'And this one is *all* yours,' she said. 'Here's your room. I do hope you'll like it.' She took him into a small but charming front bedroom, switching on the light as she went in.

'The morning sun comes right in the window, Mr Perkins. It is Mr Perkins, isn't it?'

'No,' he said. 'It's Weaver,'

'Mr Weaver. How nice. I've put a water-bottle between the sheets to air them out, Mr Weaver. It's such a comfort to have a hot water-bottle in a strange bed with clean sheets, don't you agree? And you may light the gas fire at any time if you feel chilly.' [44]

'Thank you,' Billy said. 'Thank you ever so much.' He noticed that the bedspread had been taken off the bed, and that the bedclothes had been neatly turned back on one side, all ready for someone to get in.

'I'm so glad you appeared,' she said, looking earnestly [45] into his face. 'I was beginning to get worried.'

'That's all right,' Billy answered brightly. 'You mustn't worry about me.' He put his suitcase on the chair and started to open it.

'And what about supper, my dear? Did you manage to get anything to eat before you came here?'

'I'm not a bit hungry, thank you,' he said. 'I think I'll just go to bed as soon as possible because tomorrow I've got to get up rather early and report to the office.'

'Very well, then. I'll leave you now so that you can unpack. [46] But before you go to bed, would you be kind enough to pop into the sitting-room on the ground floor and sign the book? Everyone has to do that because it's the law of the land, and we don't want to go breaking any laws at *this* stage in the proceedings, [47] do we?' She gave him a little wave of the hand and went quickly out of the room and closed the door.

---

44   **chilly** ['tʃɪli] : rather cold.

45   **earnestly** [ɜːnɪstli] : seriously.

46   **unpack** [ʌn'pæk] : take things out of your suitcase.

47   **at *this* stage in the proceedings** : at this point.

155   Now, the fact that his landlady appeared to be slightly off her rocker [48] didn't worry Billy in the least. After all, she was not only harmless – there was no question about that – but she was also quite obviously a kind and generous soul. He guessed that she had probably lost a son in the war, or something like that, and had never got over it.

160   So a few minutes later, after unpacking his suitcase and washing his hands, he trotted downstairs to the ground floor and entered the living-room. His landlady wasn't there, but the fire was glowing [49] in the hearth, and the little dachshund was still sleeping in front of it. The room was wonderfully warm and cosy. [50] I'm a lucky fellow, he thought, rubbing

165   his hands. This is a bit of all right.

He found the guest-book lying open on the piano, so he took out his pen and wrote down his name and address. There were only two other entries [51] above his on the page, and, as one always does with guest-books, he started to read them. One was a Christopher Mulholland from

170   Cardiff. The other was Gregory W. Temple from Bristol.

That's funny, he thought suddenly. Christopher Mulholland. It rings a bell.

Now where on earth had he heard that rather unusual name before?

Was he a boy at school? No. Was it one of his sister's numerous young

175   men, perhaps, or a friend of his father's? No, no, it wasn't any of those. He glanced down again at the book.

Christopher Mulholland   *231 Cathedral Road, Cardiff*
Gregory W. Temple   *27 Sycamore Drive, Bristol*

As a matter of fact, now he came to think of it, he wasn't at all sure

180   that the second name didn't have almost as much of a familiar ring [52] about it as the first.

'Gregory Temple?' he said aloud, searching his memory. 'Christopher Mulholland? ...'

---

48   **slightly** [slaɪtli] **off her rocker** : (sl.) a little crazy.

49   **glowing** : burning.

50   **cosy** ['kəʊzi] : comfortable and welcoming.

51   **entries** : (here) names.

52   **didn't have ... ring** : didn't sound as familiar.

'Such charming boys,' a voice behind him answered, and he turned and saw his landlady sailing into the room with a large silver tea-tray in her hands. She was holding it well out in front of her, and rather high up, as though the tray were a pair of reins [53] on a frisky [54] horse.

'They sound somehow familiar,' he said.

'They do? How interesting.'

'I'm almost positive [55] I've heard those names before somewhere. Isn't that queer? Maybe it was in the newspapers. They weren't famous in any way, were they? I mean famous cricketers or footballers or something like that?'

'Famous,' she said, setting the tea-tray down on the low table in front of the sofa. 'Oh no, I don't think they were famous. But they were extraordinarily handsome, both of them, I can promise you that. They were tall and young and handsome, my dear, just exactly like you.'

Once more, Billy glanced down at the book. 'Look here,' he said, noticing the dates. 'This last entry is over two years old.'

'It is?'

'Yes, indeed. And Christopher Mulholland's is nearly a year before that – more than *three years ago*.'

'Dear me,' she said, shaking her head and heaving a dainty [56] little sigh. 'I would never have thought it. How time does fly away from us all, doesn't it, Mr Wilkins?'

'It's Weaver,' Billy said. 'W-e-a-v-e-r.'

'Oh, of course it is!' she cried, sitting down on the sofa. 'How silly of me. I do apologize. In one ear and out the other, that's me, Mr Weaver.'

'You know something?' Billy said. 'Something that's really quite extraordinary about all this?'

'No, dear, I don't.'

'Well, you see – both of these names, Mulholland and Temple, I not only seem to remember each of them separately, so to speak, but

---

53   **reins** : long, narrow straps used to control a horse.

54   **frisky** : lively and energetic.

55   **almost positive** : almost completely certain.

56   **dainty** ['deɪntɪ] : delicate.

somehow or other, in some peculiar way, they both appear to be sort of
connected together as well. As though they were both famous for the
same sort of thing, if you see what I mean – like ... like Dempsey and
 Tunney , for example, or Churchill and Roosevelt .'

'How amusing,' she said. 'But come over here now, dear, and sit down
beside me on the sofa and I'll give you a nice cup of tea and a ginger
biscuit before you go to bed.'

'You really shouldn't bother,' Billy said. 'I didn't mean you to do
anything like that.' He stood by the piano, watching her as she fussed
about [57] with the cups and saucers. He noticed that she had small, white,
quickly moving hands, and red finger-nails.

'I'm almost positive it was in the newspapers I saw them,' Billy said.
'I'll think of it in a second. I'm sure I will.'

There is nothing more tantalizing [58] than a thing like this which
lingers [59] just outside the borders of one's memory. He hated to give up.

'Now wait a minute,' he said. 'Wait just a minute. Mulholland ...
Christopher Mulholland ... wasn't *that* the name of the Eton schoolboy
who was on a walking-tour through the West Country, and then all of a
sudden ... '

'Milk?' she said. 'And sugar?'

'Yes, please. And then all of a sudden ... '

'Eton schoolboy?' she said. 'Oh no, my dear, that can't possibly be
right because *my* Mr Mulholland was certainly not an Eton schoolboy
when he came to me. He was a Cambridge undergraduate. [60] Come over
here now and sit next to me and warm yourself in front of this lovely fire.
Come on. Your tea's all ready for you.' She patted [61] the empty place
beside her on the sofa, and she sat there smiling at Billy and waiting for
him to come over.

He crossed the room slowly, and sat down on the edge of the sofa. She
placed his teacup on the table in front of him.

---

57 **fussed** [fʌst] **about** : moved about nervously.

58 **tantalizing** ['tæntəlaɪzɪŋ] : (here) annoying, frustrating.

59 **lingers** ['lɪŋgəz] : stays.

60 **undergraduate** : college student who has not yet taken his degree.

61 **patted** : tapped gently.

'*There* we are,' she said. 'How nice and cosy this is, isn't it?'

Billy started sipping his tea. She did the same. For half a minute or so,   245
neither of them spoke. But Billy knew that she was looking at him. Her
body was half-turned towards him, and he could feel her eyes resting on
his face, watching him over the rim of her teacup. Now and again, he
caught a whiff [62] of a peculiar smell that seemed to emanate directly from
her person. It was not in the least unpleasant, and it reminded him – well,   250
he wasn't quite sure what it reminded him of. Pickled [63] walnuts? New
leather? Or was it the corridors of a hospital?

Culture reference

DEMPSEY, JACK (1895-1983)	world heavyweight boxing champion who held the title from 1919 until 1926, when he was defeated by Gene Tunney
CHURCHILL, SIR WINSTON (1874-1965)	British statesman and author. Became a Member of Parliament in 1900 and was Prime Minister between 1940-45, and again between 1951-55
ROOSEVELT, FRANKLIN DELANO (1882-1945)	American statesman, President from 1933 to 1945 who met the economic crisis of the thirties with a policy called the "New Deal"

62   **whiff** [wɪf] : faint smell.
63   **Pickled** ['pɪkəld] : preserved with vinegar.

8 Have your ideas about how the story will finish changed? Look back at your answer to Activity 6.

9 Put the sentences below in the right order and correct the ones that contain factual inaccuracies.

☐ **a** The landlady confirms that the two boys were famous cricketers.

☐ **b** The two names Billy reads in the guest-book sound completely new to him.

☐ **c** The landlady says that Mr Mulholland was a Cambridge undergraduate.

☐ **d** Billy thinks that the two names are completely unrelated to each other.

☐ **e** Billy notices a strange smell but can't say exactly what it is.

☐ **f** Billy cannot remember where he had heard the two names before.

☐ **g** Billy notices that the entries in the guest-book date back to three months before.

10 Look at these two short dialogues, characterized by very short replies from the landlady. Find two other examples of this type of dialogue in this extract:

a "They sound somehow familiar," [...].
"They do? How interesting."

b "This last entry is over two years old."
"It is?"

c ....
....

d ....
....

What impression do these short dialogues give of the landlady?

11 The landlady seems to appreciate certain "qualities" in her guests
    (see below). How does she describe Christopher Mulholland and
    Gregory Temple? What comparisons does she draw between them
    and Billy? Skim the part you have just read and fill in the blanks
    (complete Part 5 as you read the next section).

    Part 3:   "... an acceptable young gentleman ..."

              "... someone who is just *exactly* right [...] like you"

    Part 4:   ....
              ....

    Part 5:   ....
              ....

'Mr Mulholland was a great one for his tea,' she said at length. 'Never in my life have I seen anyone drink as much tea as dear, sweet Mr
255   Mulholland.'

'I suppose he left fairly recently,' Billy said. He was still puzzling his head about the two names. He was positive now that he had seen them in the newspapers – in the headlines.

'Left?' she said, arching her brows. 'But my dear boy, he never left.
260   He's still here. Mr Temple is also here. They're on the third floor, both of them together.'

Billy set down his cup slowly on the table, and stared at his landlady. She smiled back at him, and then she put out one of her white hands and patted him comfortingly on the knee. 'How old are you, my dear?' she
265   asked.

'Seventeen.'

'Seventeen!' she cried. 'Oh, it's the perfect age! Mr Mulholland was also seventeen. But I think he was a trifle [65] shorter than you are, in fact I'm sure he was, and his teeth weren't *quite* so white. You have the most
270   beautiful teeth, Mr Weaver, did you know that?'

'They're not as good as they look,' Billy said. 'They've got simply masses [66] of fillings in them at the back.'

'Mr Temple, of course, was a little older,' she said, ignoring his remark. 'He was actually twenty-eight. And yet I never would have
275   guessed it if he hadn't told me, never in my whole life. There wasn't a *blemish* [67] on his body.'

'A what?' Billy said.

'His skin was *just* like a baby's.'

There was a pause. Billy picked up his teacup and took another sip of
280   his tea, then he set it down again gently in its saucer. He waited for her to say something else, but she seemed to have lapsed [68] into another of her silences. He sat there staring straight ahead of him into the far corner of the room, biting his lower lip.

---

65   **a trifle** ['traɪfəl] : (idm) a little.

66   **masses** ['mæsɪz] : (infml) lots.

67   *blemish* : imperfection.

68   **have lapsed** [læpst] : have fallen.

'That parrot,' he said at last. 'You know something? It had me completely fooled [69] when I first saw it through the window from the street. I could have sworn it was alive.'

'Alas, no longer.'

'It's most terribly clever the way it's been done,' he said. 'It doesn't look in the least bit dead. Who did it?'

'I did.'

'*You* did?'

'Of course,' she said. 'And have you met my little Basil as well?' She nodded towards the dachshund curled up so comfortably in front of the fire. Billy looked at it. And suddenly, he realized that this animal had all the time been just as silent and motionless as the parrot. He put out a hand and touched it gently on the top of its back. The back was hard and cold, and when he pushed the hair to one side with his fingers, he could see the skin underneath, greyish-black and dry and perfectly preserved.

'Good gracious me,' he said. 'How absolutely fascinating.' He turned away from the dog and stared with deep admiration at the little woman beside him on the sofa. 'It must be most awfully difficult to do a thing like that.'

'Not in the least,' she said. 'I stuff [70] *all* my little pets myself when they pass away. [71] Will you have another cup of tea?'

'No, thank you,' Billy said. The tea tasted faintly [72] of bitter almonds, and he didn't much care for it.

'You did sign the book, didn't you?'

'Oh, yes.'

'That's good. Because later on, if I happen to forget what you were called, then I can always come down here and look it up. I still do that almost every day with Mr Mulholland and Mr ... Mr ... '

'Temple,' Billy said. 'Gregory Temple. Excuse my asking, but haven't there been *any* other guests here except them in the last two or three years?'

---

69 **fooled** [fuːld] : deceived.

70 **stuff** [stʌf] : fill (to restore their original shape and to preserve them).

71 **pass away** : (euphemism) die.

72 **faintly** [feɪntli] : slightly.

315   Holding her teacup high in one hand, inclining her head slightly to the left, she looked up at him out of the corners of her eyes and gave him another gentle little smile.

'No, my dear,' she said. 'Only you.'

12 Explain the ending of the story in your own words. What do you think will happen to Billy? Did the ending surprise you or not?

13 Find a suitable moral for the story.

Now reconsider the story as a whole.

14 A story can have an open ending (when it is left to the reader to imagine how the story will finish) or a closed ending (when all the elements of a story are brought together to form a conclusion and any problems are resolved). In "The Landlady" the author does not describe the end of the story, yet the reader is made to feel that there is no doubt about what is going to happen.

Can you identify the phrases or words that hint at the outcome of the story? Write them in the space below (an example has been given).

"... he was a tiny bit frightened of them." (*ll. 54-5*)

....

....

....

....

15 The author's skill in stories like "The Landlady" also lies in his ability to mislead the reader. Answer the following questions.

    a In what ways was the ending unpredictable? Identify the elements in the story which are designed to "reassure" the reader about the landlady (for example "She looked exactly like the mother of one's best school-friend ...")

    b What is the effect of this reassuring presentation of the landlady?
- it makes the ending more of a shock
- it creates a false sense of security
- other

16 "The bedclothes had been neatly turned back on one side, all ready for someone to get in." The air of quiet expectancy in the house is in direct contrast to the air of busyness that the landlady gives. Find words, expressions and similes that the author uses to create this impression.

17 How does the author build up suspense in "The Landlady"? Read the statements below and say which one you agree with. Find evidence in the text to support your choice.

    a by arranging the plot in a particular way: events are not presented in chronological order

    b the story is told in such a way as to arouse curiosity: certain facts are hidden and have to be worked out by the reader

    c we see events through Billy's eyes we do not have access to the landlady's thoughts

    d by creating the feeling that something unexpected is going to happen

    e clues hinting at the landlady's real motives are cleverly scattered throughout the text

    f the pace of narration occasionally slows down to create a build-up of tension and suspense

    g the pace of narration is quick: the style is concise and everything happens quickly

18 Now study the lexical features of the story.

    a Cohesion in a text is created by devices such as repetition, synonyms or words belonging to the same semantic group. In the short story you have read there are several examples of lexical cohesion. Can you identify some of them? You may start by focusing on lines 18-24, then quickly scan the whole story for further examples.

    b "**Intensifiers**" are adverbs of degree which can be used to make an adjective "stronger" eg. "incredibly good". Here is a list of adverbs from the story. Find them in the text and decide whether they function as intensifiers or not.

		intensifiers	not intensifiers
briskly	(l. 20)	☐	☐
fantastically	(l. 93)	☐	☐
terribly	(l. 101)	☐	☐
exactly	(l. 121)	☐	☐
earnestly	(l. 140)	☐	☐
brightly	(l. 142)	☐	☐
quickly	(l. 154)	☐	☐
wonderfully	(l. 164)	☐	☐
extraordinarily	(l. 196)	☐	☐
comfortingly	(l. 264)	☐	☐

What effect do these adverbs produce?

19 How does the structure of "The Landlady" differ from the more traditional structure of a short story, where there is a central climax followed by a conclusion?

20 Focus on particular graphological features used in this story, ie. words in italics. What is the effect of these devices? Tick the following suggestions as you think appropriate:

- to draw the reader's attention to a particular word
- to provide the reader with clues as to the real nature of things
- to stress any ambiguity in the situation
- to stress irony
- to convey on page what in everyday speech is conveyed by mimicry, intonation etc.
- to get the reader to participate in the character's experience

21 From the list of themes given below, tick the one you think most appropriate to the story or add your own suggestions.

- madness
- the grotesque
- preserving beauty
- naivety
- judging by appearances
- the contrast between appearance and reality
- other

22 How would you describe the language used in the story? Find examples in the text to support your ideas.

- realistic
- everyday
- polite
- elevated
- conventional
- straightforward
- complimentary
- colloquial

Beyond the text

Activity

Imagine you are a journalist reporting on Billy's sudden disappearance. Choose either **A** or **B** and write an article where you include a physical description and all the information you know about him.

A   A witness has greatly helped the police with details which may help to solve the case! S/he was taking her/his dog for its usual evening walk when s/he saw a young man entering the boarding house!

B   Apart from the porter at the station, nobody seems to have noticed the young man. Inspector Martin is working hard on the case but unfortunately without much success! It looks as if this case might remain unsolved.

Talking points

People kill for many reasons. In "The Landlady", perhaps, it was the notion of preserving beauty or it was just madness ...

Read the article on the following page. Is there any apparent reason for Alan Hall's crime?

Dreams drove sadist to kill

A SADIST who for years had dreamt of killing was sent to Rampton high-security hospital yesterday after admitting that he strangled and stabbed his girlfriend.

After killing Zacherley Brynin, Alan Hall, 29, told police: "It is a relief having murdered someone, you know. I have often thought about killing someone. I knew I would do it for ages but it was not planned, it just happened." He claimed that he had told a psychiatrist who had treated him for an alcohol problem that he was going to kill, "but he would not listen".

Hall, from Regent's Park, central London, had denied murdering Miss Brynin, 22, on June 29 last year but admitted manslaughter [1] on the grounds of diminished responsibility. His plea was accepted after the court was told that three psychiatrists agreed he suffered from a severe psychopathic disorder of a sexual and sadistic nature. "You are a grave and immediate danger to others," Judge Denison, Common Serjeant in the City of London, said at the Old Bailey.

He ordered that Hall be sent to Rampton for assessment over 12 weeks, adding: "I do not know whether your condition is susceptible to medical treatment and until I do I cannot dispose of the case."

Miss Brynin, whose mother lives in Hampstead, north-west London, and father in Belgium, had wanted to become a model. She absconded [2] from a halfway house [3] where she was receiving treatment for schizophrenia and within days moved into Hall's home.

Hall told police that she had

Zacherley Brynin: was strangled and stabbed

done nothing to provoke him.

He said he had been overcome by waves of violence over five years, mainly towards strangers in the street. "I have often had thoughts of killing in my mind."

(from THE TIMES)

---

1   **manslaughter** ['mæn,slɔːtər] : unintentional killing.

2   **absconded** : ran away secretly; escaped.

3   **halfway house** : a house where recently released prisoners, or patients with mental illness can stay while preparing to return to normal life.

REMOTE

by BERNARD MACLAVERTY

BERNARD MACLAVERTY was born in Belfast in 1945 where he spent his childhood and early youth. After taking his degree in English at Queen's University, he left Ireland and moved first to Edinburgh and then to the island of Islay, off the west coast of Scotland.

He has written two widely acclaimed novels: *Lamb* (1980) and *Cal* (1983), both made into films, where the tragedy of Northern Ireland is the source of inspiration. *Cal*, in particular, deals with political violence, Irish nationalism and terrorism.

He also wrote three collections of short stories: *Secrets, A Time to Dance* and *The Great Profundo*, where he examines the themes of religion, violence, sectarianism, innocence and age.

He lives in Glasgow with his family and is a full-time writer.

Before reading

1 What do you associate with the word "remote"? Would you use this word to describe a feeling, a place, a memory, an event, a person or something else?

2 The story you are going to read is set at Christmas time. What feelings do you associate with that time of year? Can you think of a possible connection between the title and Christmas?

3 Listen to the first part of the story, and answer the following questions:

  a where and when is the story set?

  b how many characters are introduced?

4 Now read the text and fill in the table on page 53.

A ROUND about the end of each month she would write a letter, but because it was December she used an old Christmas card, which she found at the bottom of the biscuit tin among her pension books. She stood dressed in her outdoor clothes on tiptoe at the bedroom window waiting for the   5
bird-watcher's ¹ Land Rover to come over the top of the hill two miles away. When she saw it she dashed ² slamming ³ the door after her and running in her stiff-legged ⁴ fashion down the lane on to the road. Her aim was to be walking, breathing normally, when the Land Rover would indicate and stop in the middle of the one-track road.   10

---

1 **bird-watcher** : person who studies birds in their natural surroundings.

2 **dashed** : ran quickly.

3 **slamming** [slæmɪŋ] : shutting forcefully.

4 **stiff-legged** ['stɪf'legd] : rigid.

'Can I give you a lift?'

'Aye.'

She walked round the front of the shuddering [5] engine and climbed up
to sit on the split [6] seat. Mushroom-coloured foam bulged from [7] its crack. [8]
15   More often than not she had to kick things aside to make room for her feet.
It was not the lift she would have chosen but it was all there was. He
shoved [9] the wobbling [10] stick through the gears and she had to shout – each
month the same thing.

'Where are you for?'

20   'The far side.'

'I'm always lucky just to catch you.'

He was dressed like one of those hitch-hikers, green khaki jacket, cord [11]
trousers and laced-up mountain boots. His hair was long and unwashed
and his beard divided into points like the teats of a goat.

25   'Are you going as far as the town this time?'

'Yes.'

'Will you drop me off.'

'Sure. Christmas shopping?'

'Aye, that'll be right.'

---

5   **shuddering** : vibrating violently.

6   **split** : broken, cut.

7   **bulged** [bʌldʒd] **from** : swelled out from.

8   **crack** : line where it was broken.

9   **shoved** [ʃʌvd] : pushed roughly.

10   **wobbling** ['wɒblɪŋ] : moving unsteadily.

11   **cord** : (abbr. of corduroy) thick cloth with vertical ridges.

CHARACTERS	APPEARANCE	ACTION
Woman		
Man		

What impression of the woman's character and lifestyle have you been able to form so far?

5 Listen to the next section and decide if the statements given below are true or false.

		True	False
a	The man complains about the fact that there aren't as many birds on the island as there used to be.	☐	☐
b	He is from Birmingham and has come to the island to do some bird-watching.	☐	☐
c	The woman is a native of the island.	☐	☐
d	Her husband was killed in a car accident.	☐	☐
e	He was a taxi driver.	☐	☐
f	At the Post Office she collects her pension and posts her card.	☐	☐
g	She does some shopping.	☐	☐
h	She decides to visit Mary and have a chat with her.	☐	☐

Now read the text and check your answers. Then correct the false statements.

30   The road spun [12] past, humping [13] and squirming [14] over peat bogs, [15] the single track bulging at passing places – points which were marked by tall black and white posts to make them stand out against the landscape. Occasionally in the bog there were incisions, a black-brown colour, herring-boned [16] with scars [17] where peat had been cut.

35   'How's the birds doing?' she shouted.

'Fine. I've never had so many as this year.'

His accent was English and it surprised her that he had blackheads [18] dotting his cheekbones and dirty hands.

'Twenty-two nesting pairs [19] – so far.'

40   'That's nice.'

'Compared with sixteen last year.'

'What are they?'

He said what they were but she couldn't hear him properly. They joined the main road and were silent for a while. Then rounding a corner

45   the bird-man suddenly applied the brakes. [20] Two cars, facing in opposite directions, sat in the middle of the road, their drivers having a conversation. The bird-man muttered [21] and steered [22] round them, the Land Rover tilting [23] as it mounted the verge. [24]

'I'd like to see them try that in Birmingham.'

50   'Is that where you're from?'

He nodded.

12   **spun** : moved along rapidly.

13   **humping** ['hʌmpɪŋ] : going up and down (the surface of the road was uneven).

14   **squirming** ['skwɜːmɪŋ] : twisting, writhing.

15   **peat** [piːt] **bogs** : marshy areas.

16   **herring-boned** : in a zigzag pattern.

17   **scars** [skɑːz] : marks left on the skin by a wound.

18   **blackheads** ['blækhedz] : small, black, blocked skin pores.

19   **nesting pairs** : pairs (of birds) building and sharing a nest.

20   **brakes** [breɪks] : device for reducing the speed of or stopping a vehicle.

21   **muttered** ['mʌtəd] : said something in a low voice.

22   **steered** ['stɪəd] : moved the vehicle (in a particular direction).

23   **tilting** : inclining.

24   **verge** : (here) roadside.

'Why did you come to the island?'

'The birds.'

'Aye, I suppose there's not too many down there.'

He smiled and pointed to an open packet of Polo mints on the   55
dashboard. [25] She lifted them and saw that the top sweet was soiled, the
relief letters almost black. She prised [26] it out and gave it to him. The
white one beneath she put in her mouth.

'Thanks,' she said.

'You born on the island?'   60

'City born and bred.' She snorted. [27] 'I was lured [28] here by a man
forty-two years ago.'

'I never see him around.'

'I'm not surprised. He's dead this long time.' She cracked the ring of
the mint between her teeth.   65

'I'm sorry.'

She chased [29] the two crescents of mint [30] around with her tongue.

'What did he do?'

'He drowned himself. [31] In the loch.'

'I'm sorry, I didn't mean that.'   70

'On Christmas Day. He was mad in the skull – away with the fairies.'

There was a long pause in which he said again that he was sorry. Then
he said, 'What I meant was – what did he do for a living?'

'What does it matter now?'

The bird-man shook his head and concentrated on the road ahead.   75

'He was a shepherd,' she said. Then a little later, 'He was the driver.
There should always be one in the house who can drive.'

25   **dashboard** ['dæʃ'bɔːd] : the control panel (below windscreen) of a car.

26   **prised** [praɪzd] : removed carefully, but with difficulty.

27   **snorted** : forced air out through her nose as an expression of contempt and
        surprise. (She thinks the question is unnecessary.)

28   **lured** : attracted (as if into a trap).

29   **chased** [tʃeɪst] : (here) played with.

30   **crescents of mints** : two halves of a polo.

31   **drowned** [draʊnd] **himself** : killed himself (by immersing himself in water).

He let her off at the centre of the village and she had to walk the steep hill to the Post Office. She breathed through her mouth and took a rest halfway up, holding on to a small railing. Distances grew with age.

Inside she passed over her pension book, got her money and bought a first-class stamp. She waited until she was outside before she took the letter from her bag. She licked the stamp, stuck it on the envelope and dropped it in the letter box. Walking down the hill was easier.

She went to the Co-op to buy sugar and tea and porridge. The shop was strung [32] with skimpy [33] tinselled decorations [34] and the music they were playing was Christmas hits – 'Rudolf' and 'I saw Mammy Kissing Santa Claus'. She only had a brief word with Elizabeth at the check-out because of the queue behind her. In the butcher's she bought herself a pork chop and some bacon. His bacon lasted longer than the packet stuff.

When she had her shopping finished she wondered what to do to pass the time. She could visit young Mary but if she did that she would have to talk. Not having enough things to say she felt awkward [35] listening to the tick of the clock and the distant cries of sea birds. Chat was a thing you got out of the habit of when you were on your own all the time and, beside, Mary was shy. Instead she decided to buy a cup of tea in the café. And treat herself to an almond bun. She sat near the window where she could look out for the post van.

---

32   **strung** [strʌŋ] : (here) decorated.

33   **skimpy** : inadequate, not sufficient.

34   **tinselled decorations** : glittering shiny decorations.

35   **awkward** ['ɔːkwəd] : embarrassed, uneasy.

6   Focus on the lines given below and say what we learn about the
    woman's feelings towards her husband. Discuss in pairs.

    • "City born and bred." She snorted. "I was lured here by a man
      forty-two years ago." *(ll. 61-2)*
    • "He was mad in the skull – away with the fairies." *(l. 71)*
    • "He was the driver. There should always be one in the house who
      can drive." *(ll. 76-7)*

    Now choose the adjectives from the list below, that you think best
    describe the way the woman feels about her husband.

    • resentful   • detached   • patronizing
    • nostalgic   • affectionate   • proud
    • respectful   • unkind   • irritated
    • uncomfortable   • loving   • indifferent

7   What details about the bird-man strike the woman as unexpected
    and unpleasant?

8   Focus on the line "she waited until she was outside ....". Why do you
    think she does so? Discuss in pairs.

9   Choose from the list of adjectives below (or use your own) those you
    think could describe the woman. Find evidence in the text to back up
    your choice(s).

    • proud   • single-minded   • tidy   • lonely
    • practical   • sociable   • impractical   • down-to-earth
    • cynical   • sensitive   • strange   • disillusioned
    • resigned   • superior   • dignified   • frustrated

10 The section you have just read ends: "She sat near the window where
    she could look out for the post van." Why do you think she is looking
    out for the post van? Discuss in pairs. Then listen to the last part of the
    story and compare your predictions with the actual ending of the
    story. Were they right?

11 Read the text and answer the questions.

   a Identify the lines where a flashback occurs.

- What information do you learn?
- Do you get any further insight into the woman's feelings or are your previous impressions confirmed?

   b Who do you think she sends the letter to?

       The café was warm and it, too, was decorated. Each time the door
100   opened the hanging fronds of tinsel fluttered. [36] On a tape somewhere
carols were playing. Two children, sitting with their mother, were
playing with a new toy car on the table-top. The cellophane wrapping
had been discarded [37] on the floor. They both imitated engine noises
although only one of them was pushing it round the plates. The other sat
105   waiting impatiently for his turn.
       She looked away from them and stared into her tea. When they dredged
him up [38] on Boxing Day he had two car batteries tied to his wrists. He was
nothing if not thorough. [39] One of them had been taken from his own van
parked by the loch shore and the thing had to be towed [40] to the garage. If
110   he had been a drinking man he could have been out getting drunk or fallen
into bad company. But there was only the black depression. All that day
the radio had been on to get rid of the dread. [41]
       When 'Silent Night' came on the tape and the children started to
squabble over [42] whose turn it was she did not wait to finish her tea but
115   walked slowly to the edge of the village with her bag of shopping, now

     36   **fluttered** ['flʌtəd] : moved about (in an irregular way).

     37   **discarded** : (here) abandoned.

     38   **dredged** [dredʒd] **him up** : brought him to the surface of water.

     39   **thorough** ['θʌrə] : meticulous.

     40   **towed** [təʊd] : pulled along with a rope or chain.

     41   **dread** : great fear, terror.

     42   **squabble** ['skwɒbl] **over** : quarrel noisily.

and again pausing to look over her shoulder. The scarlet of the post van caught her eye and she stood on the verge with her arm out. When she saw it was Stuart driving she smiled. He stopped the van and she ducked down [43] to look in the window.

'Anything for me today?'   120

He leaned across to the basket of mail which occupied the passenger seat position and began to rummage [44] through the bundles of letters and cards held together with elastic bands.

'This job would be all right if it wasn't for bloody Chistmas.' He paused at her single letter. 'Aye, there's just one.'   125

'Oh good. You might as well run me up, seeing as you're going that way.'

He sighed and looked over his shoulder at a row of houses.

'Wait for me round the corner.'

She nodded and walked on ahead while he made some deliveries. The   130 lay-by [45] was out of sight of the houses and she set [46] her bag down to wait. Stuart seemed to take a long time. She looked down at the loch in the growing dark. The geese were returning for the night, filling the air with their squawking. [47] They sounded like a dance-hall full of people laughing and enjoying themselves, heard from a distance on the night wind.

---

43   **ducked down** : moved down quickly.

44   **rummage** [rʌmɪdʒ] : look for something (in a disordered way).

45   **lay-by** ['leɪ'baɪ] : parking space at the side of the road.

46   **set** : put.

47   **squawking** ['skwɔːkɪŋ] : (esp. birds) loud harsh cry.

Now reconsider the story as a whole.

12 There are two settings in this story, the countryside and the village.

    a Look at the description of the country in lines 30-4. Which verbs are used to describe the road? Are they dynamic or static? What do they suggest?
How is the bog described (think about nouns and adjectives)?
Is it described in positive, negative or neutral words? What is the combined effect of the descriptions of the road and the bog?

      • The landscape is described with positive images and language – the woman identifies with it.

      • The landscape is described negatively. The language used suggests harshness – the woman does not feel any affinity with it.

      • Other

    In the light of your answer to the above question, how would you define the journey to town?

      • uncomfortable and tortuous

      • exciting

      • smooth and pleasant

    Think in terms of analogy and symbols; what could the woman's journey stand for? Discuss.

    b Study the lines below describing aspects of village life.
      lines 85-9   lines 99-101   lines 132-6

      • What aspects of the life in this village are emphasized?

      • What is the effect of this description? Read the following suggestions and say which one you agree with.

        – The village acts as a foil to the woman's loneliness.

        – It parallels the woman's mood because she is at one with her surroundings.

        – It contributes to creating a particular atmosphere in the story but has no evident connection to the woman.

13 MacLaverty's language has been called precise and detailed, his dialogues realistic. Do you think such a description could apply to "Remote"? Back up your answer with examples from the text.

14 Compare and contrast the opening scene and the ending. Is the same scene repeated? In the light of your answer to this question how would you define the structure of the story?

15 Where do you think the author's main interests lie?

- in conveying a particular mood
- in portraying credible characters
- in developing a theme
- in arranging incidents in a crescendo to create a climax

16 In this story the reader has to work out much of the meaning and background information and the language has to be studied carefully to understand what lies below the surface and have a more complete picture of the character. Read the statements given below and say which one(s) you agree with.

- the woman clearly regrets having wasted opportunities in her life
- she didn't have a fulfilling married life
- she feels superior to the islanders
- she wants to be respected and keep up pretences
- she does not feel at ease with the environment around her
- she enjoys being on her own
- she doesn't mind being alone
- she lives in the past
- she longs for the affection she does not have
- she invents her own affections

17 What do you think the main themes in the story are?

Beyond the text

Activity 1

Imagine you are the woman when she was younger. Write a page of her diary describing either the time she spent in her native town or her first years on the island.

....
....
....
....
....
....
....
....

Activity 2

The story doesn't provide a physical description of the woman. How do you imagine her? Bearing in mind her psychological traits write a few lines describing her appearance.

....
....
....
....
....

Talking points

1   In literature the theme of the island is widely exploited. It has been variously used as a symbol to represent escape/freedom/adventure/disaster/exile/savagery etc. Can you think of any examples where this theme has been explored in a book or poem you have read? Discuss in class.

2   The problem of loneliness is dealt with in the article given below. What aspects of loneliness does this article focus on?

More families dump[1] granny for Christmas

by Anna Blundy

AN 85-year-old woman lay in the casualty department of London's Whittington hospital last week calling for her father. "I don't know where I am," she moaned. "Am I dead?" She was diagnosed as suffering from chronic confusion and taken to the geriatric ward, a victim of the seasonal spate[2] of "granny dumping".

Over the festive period, Britain's hospitals have been deluged with elderly patients admitted with problems ranging from the near-fatal to the trivial. What many have in common is a search for a Christmas refuge. Some admit themselves out of loneliness and desperation. Others reach hospital after falling over, slight injuries complicated because their professional helpers have left them to fend for themselves[3] over the holidays. But a growing number are brought in to be dumped by frustrated families who have reached the end of their tether.[4]

Gwen Sayers, a geriatrician at London's Homerton hospital, says home care breaks down over the holidays. "I don't even try to discharge anyone until after the new year because elderly patients need care that we can't arrange while everyone else is away enjoying themselves."

However, Dr Gerald Bennett, of the Royal hospital in the East End, suspects many families granny-dump at Christmas as a desperate attempt to get long-awaited medical care. "Anguished relatives feel they need to confront the system," he said.

Across Britain, hospital staff deplore the state of geriatric care at home and in the community. Sarah Fowles, staff nurse on the geriatrics ward at Hope hospital in Manchester, said: "It is really sad. They will come in with something minor like a chest infection and then that gets resolved and you are stuck with a social problem because the family won't take them and everything is closed for the holiday. We can't just send them home on their own."

(from THE SUNDAY TIMES)

1   **dump** : leave, abandon.

2   **spate** : large number, amount.

3   **fend for themselves** : look after themselves.

4   **reached the end of their tether** : have no patience or energy left.

JUBILEE

by GRAHAM GREENE

GRAHAM GREENE was born in 1904 in Berkhamsted, Hertfordshire. He was educated at the school where his father was headmaster and then at Balliol College, Oxford. In 1926 he joined *The Times* as a sub-editor and in the same year he converted to Catholicism.

During the war he worked for the Foreign Office and spent many years abroad, mainly in Sierra Leone, where he was stationed from 1941-43, and which provides the setting for *The Heart of the Matter* (1948).

He was a prolific writer of novels, short stories, plays and essays.

His novels include: *Brighton Rock* (1938), *The End of the Affair* (1951), *Our Man in Havana* (1958), *The Honorary Consul* (1973), *Doctor Fischer of Geneva* (1980). His works contain an unusual combination of adventure and introspection, of exoticism and moral or religious conflict.

He died in 1991.

Before reading

1 Jubilee is the celebration of a special anniversary or event occurring every 25 or 50 years (ie. the Silver Jubilee is the 25th anniversary of the Queen coming to the throne). What atmosphere do you think this story called "Jubilee" will have? In pairs write down as many words and expressions you can think of which are connected with the word 'jubilee'.

2 Read the first part of the story and fill in the table on page 69.

M R CHALFONT ironed his trousers and his tie. Then he folded up [1] his ironing-board and put it away. He was tall and he had preserved his figure; he looked distinguished even in his pants in the small furnished bed-sitting room he kept off Shepherd's Market. He was fifty, 5 but he didn't look more than forty-five; he was stony broke, [2] but he remained unquestionably Mayfair .

He examined his collar with anxiety; he hadn't been out of doors for more than a week, except to the public-house at the corner to eat his morning and evening ham roll, and then he always wore an overcoat and 10 a soiled [3] collar. He decided that it wouldn't damage the effect if he wore it once more; he didn't believe in economizing too rigidly over his laundry, [4] you had to spend money in order to earn money, but there was no point in being extravagant. [5] And somehow he didn't believe in his

---

1   **folded** ['fəʊldɪd] **up** : closed.
2   **stony broke** : (sl.) entirely without money, penniless.
3   **soiled** [sɔɪld] : dirty.
4   **economizing ... his laundry** ['lɔːndri] : saving money on the washing and/or cleaning of his clothes.
5   **in being extravagant** [ɪk'strævəgənt] : in spending excessive amounts of money.

15 luck this cocktail time; he was going out for the good of his morale, [6] because after a week away from the restaurants it would have been so easy to let everything slide, to confine himself to his room and his twice daily visit to the public-house.

20 The Jubilee decorations were still out in the cold windy May. Soiled by showers and soot [7] the streamers [8] blew up across Piccadilly, draughty [9] with desolation. They were the reminder of a good time Mr Chalfont hadn't shared; he hadn't blown whistles [10] or thrown paper ribbons; [11] he certainly hadn't danced to any harmoniums. His neat figure was like a symbol of Good Taste as he waited with folded umbrella for the traffic

25 lights to go green; he had learned to hold his hand so that one frayed [12] patch on his sleeve didn't show, and the rather exclusive club tie, freshly ironed, might have been bought that morning. It wasn't lack of patriotism or loyalty which had kept Mr Chalfont indoors all through Jubilee week. Nobody drank the toast [13] of the King more sincerely than Mr Chalfont so

30 long as someone else was standing [14] the drink, but an instinct deeper than good form had warned him [15] not to be about. Too many people whom he had once known (so he explained it) were coming up from the country; they might want to look him up, and a fellow just couldn't ask them back to a room like this. That explained his discretion; it didn't

35 explain his sense of oppression while he waited for the Jubilee to be over.
Now he was back at the old game.

6   **morale** [mə'rɑːl] : state of mind.

7   **soot** [sʊt] : black powder produced from a coal fire.

8   **streamers** : narrow strips of coloured paper put across a street (room, door) as decoration.

9   **draughty** [drɑːfti] : (here) cold and windy.

10   **whistles** ['wɪslz] : instruments which make a high-pitched sound when air is blown through them.

11   **paper ribbons** : narrow strips of paper for decoration.

12   **frayed** [freɪd] : worn.

13   **drank the toast** : drank to the health of.

14   **standing** : paying for.

15   **warned** [wɔːnd] **him** : put him on his guard.

Jubilee

Culture reference

MAYFAIR a fashionable and expensive area in the West End of London, characterized by high-class shops, restaurants and hotels

MR CHALFONT	**Age** .... **Physical details** ....
SETTING	**Where** .... **When** ....

3 Why did Mr Chalfont stay indoors during the Jubilee celebrations? (Skim *ll. 27-35*).

4 What do you think "the old game" is? Discuss in pairs.

5 Read the next part of the story. Check your answer to Activity 4 and fill in the table on page 72.

He called it that himself, smoothing [16] his neat grey military moustache. The old game. Somebody going rapidly round the corner into Berkeley Street nudged [17] him playfully and said, 'Hullo, you old devil,' and was gone again, leaving the memory of many playful nudges in the   40

16   **smoothing** ['smuːðɪŋ] : making flat with the fingers.
17   **nudged** [nʌdʒd]: touched lightly with elbow.

old days, of Merdy and the Boob. For he couldn't disguise [18] the fact that he was after the ladies. He didn't want to disguise it. It made his whole profession appear even to himself rather gallant and carefree. [19] It disguised the fact that the ladies were not so young as they might be and that it was the ladies (God bless them!) who paid. It disguised the fact that Merdy and the Boob had long ago vanished from his knowledge. The list of his acquaintances [20] included a great many women but hardly a single man; no one was more qualified by a long grimy [21] experience to tell smoking-room stories , but the smoking-room in which Mr Chalfont was welcome did not nowadays exist.

Mr Chalfont crossed the road. It wasn't an easy life, it exhausted him nervously and physically, he needed a great many sherries [22] to keep going. The first sherry he had always to pay for himself; that was the thirty pounds he marked as expenses on his income-tax return. He dived [23] through the entrance, not looking either way, for it would never do for the porter to think that he was soliciting [24] any of the women who moved heavily like seals through the dim aquarium light of the lounge. But his usual seat was occupied.

He turned away to look for another chair where he could exhibit himself discreetly: the select tie, the tan, the grey distinguished hair, the strong elegant figure, the air of a retired Governor from the Colonies. He studied the woman who sat in his chair covertly: [25] he thought he'd seen her somewhere, the mink coat, [26] the overblown [27] figure, the expensive dress. Her face was familiar but unnoted, [28] like that of someone you pass

18 **disguise** [dɪsgaɪz] : hide.
19 **carefree** ['keəfriː] : happy, light-hearted.
20 **acquaintances** : people one knows but not on intimate terms.
21 **grimy** [graɪmi] : dirty.
22 **sherries** : glasses of strong wine from South Spain.
23 **dived** [daɪvd] : (here) threw himself head first (usually into water).
24 **soliciting** [sə'lɪsɪtɪŋ] : making sexual advances to.
25 **covertly** ['kəʊvɜːtli] : secretly.
26 **mink coat** : coat made from the thick brown fur of the mink (a small animal).
27 **overblown** [əʊvə'bləʊn] : excessively elaborate.
28 **unnoted** : not special.

every day at the same place. She was vulgar, she was cheerful, she was 65
undoubtedly rich. He couldn't think where he had met her.

She caught Mr Chalfont's eye and winked. [29] He blushed, he was
horrified, nothing of this sort had ever happened to him before; the
porter was watching and Mr Chalfont felt scandal at his elbow, [30] robbing
him of his familiar restaurant, his last hunting ground, turning him 70
perhaps out of Mayfair altogether into some bleak [31] Paddington parlour
where he couldn't keep up the least appearance of gallantry. [32] Am I so
obvious, [33] he thought, so obvious? He went hastily across to her before
she could wink again. 'Excuse me,' he said, 'you must remember me.
What a long time ...' 75

Culture reference

SMOKING-ROOM STORIES	stories told after dinner in the once common private gentlemen's clubs (in a room set aside for smoking)
PADDINGTON	a low-income area just outside the West End

29 **winked** [wɪŋkt] : closed one eye quickly, to convey a private signal.

30 **at his elbow** : (here) very near, imminent.

31 **bleak** [bliːk] : depressing.

32 **gallantry** ['gæləntri] : (here) gentlemanly behaviour.

33 **Am I ... obvious** : Is it so easy to see what I really am?

MR CHALFONT	
His profession	
His mood	
His impression of the woman sitting in his chair	
His reaction when she winked at him	

6 What is Mr Chalfont's attitude to his profession? Look at the suggestions below and choose the one you think right.

- He is proud of his job and doesn't want to try and hide what he does.

- He doesn't mind his job, he doesn't have any particular feelings about it.

- He feels embarassed about declaring his profession but eventually comes to accept it.

- He is ashamed of his job, it causes him great suffering and is determined to give it up.

7 Go back to the beginning of the text and focus on the lines given below which all refer to Mr Chalfont, and work out possible implications as in the example given.

Example:

Reference lines	What is stressed
He always wore ... a soiled collar (*ll. 10-11*)	his sordid life

a "Nobody drank the toast ... the drink." (*ll. 29-30*)

b "The list of acquaintances ... a single man." (*ll. 46-8*)

c "He dived through the entrance ... acquarium light of the lounge." (*ll. 54-7*)

d "He turned away ... discreetly." (*ll. 59-60*)

e "He blushed ... appearance of gallantry." (*ll. 67-72*)

What can you say about Mr Chalfont's personality and social life?

8 The part you have read ends with Mr Chalfont's remark: "... you must remember me. What a long time ..." What do you expect the woman to say? How do you expect the story to develop? Discuss your ideas in pairs.

9 Now read the next part of the story and check your predictions. Decide if the statements below are true or false and correct the false ones.

	True	False
a Mr Chalfont pretends that he knows the woman and has forgotten her name, but in fact he doesn't know her.	☐	☐
b Mr Chalfont was right – the woman had lost money!	☐	☐
c The Jubilee helped Mr Chalfont to increase his income.	☐	☐
d The woman made money opening and running travel agencies.	☐	☐

'Your face is familiar, dear,' she said. 'Have a cocktail.'

'Well,' Mr Chalfont said, 'I should certainly not mind a sherry, Mrs – Mrs – I've quite forgotten your surname.'

'You're a sport,' [34] the woman said, 'but Amy will do.'

80 'Ah,' Mr Chalfont said, 'you are looking very well, Amy. It gives me much pleasure to see you sitting there again after all these – months –why, years it must be. The last time we met ...'

'I don't remember you clearly, dear, though of course when I saw you looking at me ... I suppose it was in Jermyn Street.'

85 'Jermyn Street,' Mr Chalfont said. 'Surely not Jermyn Street. I've never ... Surely it must have been when I had my flat in Curzon Street. Delectable [35] evenings one had there. I've moved since then to a rather humbler abode [36] where I wouldn't dream of inviting you ... But perhaps we could slip away to some little nest [37] of your own. Your health, my 90 dear. You look younger than ever.'

'Happy days,' Amy said. Mr Chalfont winced. [38] She fingered her mink coat. 'But you know – I've retired.'

'Ah, lost money, eh,' Mr Chalfont said. 'Dear lady, I've suffered in that way too. We must console each other a little. I suppose business is bad. 95 Your husband – I seem to recall a trying man who did his best to interfere with our idyll. It was quite an idyll, wasn't it, those evenings in Curzon Street?'

'You've got it wrong, dear. I never was in Curzon Street. But if you date back to the time I tried that husband racket, [39] why that goes years 100 back, to the mews [40] off Bond Street . Fancy your remembering. [41] It was wrong of me. I can see that now. And it never really worked. I don't think he looked like a husband. But now I've retired. Oh, no,' she said,

---

34   **You're a sport** : (here) You are too kind.

35   **Delectable** : (fml) Wonderful.

36   **abode** : (fml) home.

37   **nest** : (joc.) (here) place.

38   **winced** [wɪnst] : showed embarassment, pain on his face.

39   **racket** : (sl.) business.

40   **mews** : a row of stables converted into private residences.

41   **Fancy your remembering** : (dated) How incredible that you should have remembered.

leaning forward until he could smell the brandy on her plump [42] little lips, 'I haven't lost money, I've made it.'

'You're lucky,' Mr Chalfont said.   105

'It was all the Jubilee,' Amy explained.

'I was confined to my bed during the Jubilee,' Mr Chalfont said. 'I understand it all went off very well.'

'It was lovely,' Amy said. 'Why, I said to myself, everyone ought to do something to make it a success. So I cleaned up the streets.'   110

'I don't quite understand,' Mr Chalfont said. 'You mean the decorations?'

'No, no,' Amy said, 'that wasn't it at all. But it didn't seem to me nice, when all these Colonials [43] were in London, for them to see the girls in Bond Street and Wardour Street and all over the place. I'm proud of   115 London, and it didn't seem right to me that we should get a reputation.' [44]

'People must live.'

'Of course they must live. Wasn't I in the business myself, dear?'

'Oh,' Mr Chalfont said, 'you were in the business?' It was quite a shock to him; he looked quickly this way and that, fearing that he might have   120 been observed.

'So you see I opened a House and split with the girls. I took all the risk, and then of course I had my other expenses. I had to advertise.'

'How did you – how did you get it known?' He couldn't help having a kind of professional interest.   125

'Easy, dear. I opened a tourist bureau. Trips to the London underworld. Limehouse and all that. But there was always an old fellow who wanted the guide to show him something privately afterwards.'

'Very ingenious,' Mr Chalfont said.

'And loyal too, dear. It cleaned up the streets properly. Though of   130 course I only took the best. I was very select. Some of them jibbed, [45] because they said they did all the work, but as I said to them, it was My Idea.'

---

42 **plump** [plʌmp] : full, rounded.

43 **Colonials** [kə'ləʊniəlz] : British people who normally live in the colonies.

44 **reputation** : bad name.

45 **jibbed** : objected, complained.

'So now you're retired?'

135 'I made five thousand pounds, dear. It was really my jubilee as well, though you mightn't think it to look at me. I always had the makings of [46] a business woman, and I saw, you see, how I could extend the business. I opened at Brighton too. I cleaned up England in a way of speaking. It was ever so much nicer for the Colonials. There's been a lot of money in the
140 country these last weeks. Have another sherry, dear, you are looking poorly.'

'Really, really you know I ought to be going.'

'Oh, come on. It's Jubilee, isn't it? Celebrate. Be a sport.'

'I think I see a friend.'

Culture reference

BOND STREET	one of the main shopping streets of central London, famous in particular for its jewellers' and picture galleries
LIMEHOUSE	part of the East End of London, an area characterized by poverty, crime and prostitution until the 1980's

10 The expression "clean up the streets" is taken literally by Mr Chalfont, who fails to understand the euphemism. What is the effect of this misunderstanding?

- to break up the tension

- to amuse the reader

- to stress Mr Chalfont's short-sightedness

- to stress the irony of the situation

- other

46   **the makings of** : the potential to be.

11 In the following section, besides getting a deeper insight into Mr Chalfont's character, the reader is also made aware of a number of contrasts between the two characters. While reading focus on these contrasts and make notes under the headings in the table below. What impression of the characters does the reader get?

MR CHALFONT	THE WOMAN
"He wilted ...."	"She bloomed..........................."
....	....
....	....
....	....
....	....
....	....
....	....

He looked helplessly around: a friend: he couldn't even think of a   145
friend's name. He wilted [47] before a personality stronger than his own.
She bloomed there like a great dressy [48] autumn flower. He felt old: my
jubilee. His frayed cuffs [49] showed; he had forgotten to arrange his hand.
He said, 'Perhaps. Just one. It ought really to be on me,' and as he
watched her bang for the waiter in the dim genteel [50] place and dominate   150
his disapproval when he came, Mr Chalfont couldn't help wondering at
the unfairness of her confidence and her health. He had a touch of
neuritis, [51] but she was carnival; [52] she really seemed to belong to the

47   **wilted** : visibly lost energy and courage.
48   **dressy** : showy.
49   **cuffs** [kʌfs] : the ends of shirt sleeves.
50   **genteel** [dʒen'tiːl] : refined.
51   **touch of neuritis** [njʊe'raɪtɪs] : slight inflammation of a nerve / nerves.
52   **carnival** : (here) high-spirited.

155 banners and drinks and plumes and processions. He said quite humbly, 'I should like to have seen the procession, but I wasn't up to it. My rheumatism,' he excused himself. His little withered [53] sense of good taste could not stand the bright plebeian spontaneity. He was a fine dancer, but they'd have outdanced him on the pavements, he made love attractively in his formal well-bred [54] way, but they'd have outloved him,

160 blind and drunk and crazy and happy in the park. He had known that he would be out of place, he'd kept away; but it was humiliating to realize that Amy had missed nothing.

12 The word 'jubilee' is used in the title of this story, but it also occurs a number of times within the story itself, sometimes with a capital 'J' when it refers to the event itself, at other times with a small 'j'. In these cases the word as it occurs acquires additional meaning. Underline the word as it occurs in the text, then explain the differences between Mr Chalfont's and the woman's 'Jubilee'.

13 Read the last section then decide which adjectives could be used to describe Mr Chalfont and the woman and write them in the table on the next page (you may choose from the adjectives given below or use your own).

- easygoing
- confident
- hypocritical
- sympathetic
- vain

- formal
- embarassed
- outspoken
- self-centred
- affected

- tactless
- patronizing
- tactful
- coarse
- self-conscious

53 **withered** ['wɪðəd] : dried up.
54 **well-bred** : refined.

MR CHALFONT	THE WOMAN

'You look properly done,[55] dear,' Amy said. 'Let me lend you a couple of quid.'[56]

'No, no,' Mr Chalfont said. 'Really I couldn't.'   165

'I expect you've given me plenty in your time.'

But had he? He couldn't remember her; it was such a long time since he'd been with a woman except in the way of business. He said, 'I couldn't. I really couldn't.' He tried to explain his attitude while she fumbled[57] in her bag.   170

'I never take money – except, you know, from friends.' He admitted desperately, 'or except in business.' But he couldn't take his eyes away. He was broke[58] and it was cruel of her to show him a five-pound note. 'No. Really.' It was a long time since his market price had been as high as five pounds.   175

'I know how it is, dear,' Amy said, 'I've been in the business myself, and I know just how you feel. Sometimes a gentleman would come home with me, give me a quid and run away as if he was scared. It was insulting. I never did like taking money for nothing.'

---

55   **properly done** : (dated, infml) (here) in serious need.

56   **quid** : (infml) pounds.

57   **fumbled** [fʌmbld] : searched awkwardly.

58   **broke** : (infml) penniless.

180   'But you're quite wrong,' Mr Chalfont said. 'That's not it at all. Not it at all.'

'Why, I could tell almost as soon as you spoke to me. You don't need to keep up pretences [59] with me, dear,' Amy went inexorably on, while Mayfair faded from his manner until there remained only the bed-sitting 185   room, the ham rolls, the iron heating on the stove. 'You don't need to be proud. But if you'd rather (it's all the same to me, it doesn't mean a thing to me) we'll go home, and let you do your stuff. [60] It's all the same to me, dear, but if you'd rather – I know how you feel,' and presently they went out together arm-in-arm into the decorated desolate street.

190   'Cheer up, dear,' Amy said, as the wind picked up the ribbons and tore them from [61] the poles and lifted the dust and made the banners flap, [62] 'a girl likes a cheerful face.' And suddenly she became raucous and merry, slapping Mr Chalfont on his back, pinching his arm, [63] saying, 'Let's have a little Jubilee spirit, dear,' taking her revenge for a world of uncongenial 195   partners on old Mr Chalfont. You couldn't call him anything else now but old Mr Chalfont.

14 In this story little happens, yet the protagonist undergoes a change in his psychology and feelings. Why does the meeting with the woman have such a devastating effect on him? Discuss.

Now reconsider the story as a whole

15 We can say that the general atmosphere of this story is established right from the start. Which grammatical and lexical features help to define the setting and the main character? Read carefully the points under each heading in the table on the following page, cross out those you don't agree with and find examples for the others.

---

59   **keep up pretences** [prɪ'tensɪz] : pretend that nothing is wrong.

60   **do your stuff** : carry out your services, ie. have sexual intercourse.

61   **tore** [tɔː] **them from** : pulled violently away from.

62   **flap** : move violently up and down or from side to side.

63   **pinching his arm** : pressing his arm between thumb and one finger.

SETTING (*ll. 19-21; 188-9*)	EXAMPLES
MOSTLY DEFINED BY: • a long and detailed description of time and place • neutral words describing facts • positively connotated words (see: **connotation**) • negatively connotated words • dynamic verbs • stative verbs	
MR CHALFONT (skim first 3 paragraphs)	EXAMPLES
MOSTLY DEFINED BY: • wide use of pronouns • verbs of perception • concrete nouns • negative verb forms • dynamic verbs • stative verbs	

What is the result of your analysis? Do you find the setting appropriate to the character. Read the list of alternatives given below and select the one you agree with. Give reasons for your choice.

- The setting is appropriate to the character: it reflects his mood and feelings.
- The setting is not particularly important in this story.
- There is a strong contrast between setting and character.

16 Some sentences from the first part of the story are echoed later in the story. Find them and write them in the lines below.

"He was fifty, but he didn't look more than forty-five."

....

"He remained unquestionably Mayfair."

....

"His neat figure was a symbol of Good Taste."

....

"He had learned to hold his hand so that one frayed patch on his sleeve didn't show."

....

What is the function of these "echoes"? Decide which of the sentences below you agree with.

- to prepare the reader for the resolution of the action
- to highlight a particular contrast or a change
- to create a particular atmosphere
- to provide clues which are essential to the understanding of the story
- to contribute to the development of the character
- to carry the plot forward
- to give the story movement
- to contribute to lexical cohesion

17 In your exercise book complete the chart below "summarizing" the main points of the story. Include line references as in the example.

BEGINNING OF THE STORY *ll. 1-49*
After a week indoors during the Jubilee celebration, Mr Chalfont gets ready to go out ...

EVENT
(something happens: another character is introduced)

FURTHER DEVELOPMENT
(consequences)

END
(modification of the character's psychology and outlook/feelings)

Now that you have studied the whole story, how would you define the structure of "Jubilee"? Give reasons for your answer.

18 Approximately half the story is written in speech mode. Can you think of any advantage of using this mode so extensively? Here are some suggestions. Select the ones you agree with or add your own and remember to back up your answers with examples from the story.

- it makes the characters come to life
- it creates ambiguity
- it makes the scene more vivid/dramatic
- it reveals aspects of the characters' personality
- it leaves greater freedom to the reader to judge characters
- it reduces the distance between the reader and the fictional world
- other

19 In spite of the great variety reporting verbs in English, the author of this short story has chosen the verb "to say" or has occasionally even omitted the reporting clause. What is the effect of this choice?

- it makes the pace of the story quicker

- it leaves the reader greater freedom of interpretation

- it allows for a greater economy of style

- other

20 Focus on the narrative perspective in this story. Read the list of statements given below and say which one(s) you agree with. Give reasons for your answer(s).

- The **point of view** is consistent throughout the story: everything is seen through Mr Chalfont's eyes.

- The **narrator** never intervenes to comment on characters or situations. He is invisible and never betrays his presence. The result is an objective account of the story.

- The narrator is clearly intrusive and his presence is felt throughout the story: he provides comments, judgements and gives explanations in the form of long digressions.

- At times events are seen from the viewpoint of the woman.

- The narrator withdraws and lets characters reveal themselves through interaction.

21 a Which character do you sympathize with most?

b What do you think of this story? Choose from the words given below (or add your own), and describe your reaction to the story. Give reasons for your answer.

- thought-provoking
- boring
- depressing
- interesting
- intriguing
- puzzling
- difficult
- unusual

Beyond the text

Activity

Imagine Amy talking to a "colleague" about her meeting with Mr Chalfont. Write a short dialogue, adding any other detail you want and try to keep the tone of the conversation informal (short sentences, elliptical forms, false starts etc.).

Talking points

1 Answer the following questions:

- What are your opinions about male prostitution?

- How much do you know about this "profession"?

- Why do most of those who practice this profession want to remain anonymous?

- Do you consider it a job just like any other?

- Do you find it socially acceptable?

- Do you think one social class may be more represented in this profession?

- Which "qualities" do you consider essential for such a "job"?
  - cynicism
  - indifference
  - exhibitionism
  - other

Have there been any developments in this profession in recent times? Think of discotheques or night clubs where men exhibit themselves, taking up roles which in the past were restricted to women (sexual provocation, stripping etc.).

2 Read this article about Anna Nicol Smith, former Playboy model, who married the elderly American millionaire Howard Marshall last year and is now a widow. What feelings do you think would be prominent in a marriage of this kind? Discuss.

Can you see any link between the article and the story you have read?

Tycoon's¹ widow in battle over will

by BEN MACINTYRE

When supermodel Anna Nicole Smith, 26, married 89-year-old super-milionaire J. Howard Marshall II last year, cynics said the world's luckiest bride would soon be one of its richest widows.

The elderly Texas oil tycoon died last weekend aged 90, and the gossip-mill is heating up for what is predicted will be a fierce battle over his $550 million (£343 million) estate between Mr Marshall's son Pierce, and Ms Smith.

Pierce Marshall won temporary guardianship of his father in February on the ground that he was "mentally incapacitated". Ms Smith was allowed to visit her ailing ² husband, but his money was held in a trust.

Ms Smith, a former check-out girl at a department store, has already been in touch with gossip columnists. Her son-in-law "never liked me", the widow told Cindy Adams of the *New York Post*, while emphasising her deep and unconditional love for her late husband. "I wasn't getting great money from him at the end ... I gave up much of my career to sit at his bedside day after day and nurse him."

As a wedding gift, Mr Marshall gave Ms Smith a Hollywood mansion and a Texas ranch but the money, she says, was never a motive.

(from THE TIMES)

1 **Tycoon** [taɪˈkuːn] : Wealthy and powerful person.
2 **ailing** [eɪlɪŋ] : ill.

DÉSIRÉE'S BABY

by Kate Chopin

KATE CHOPIN (O'Flaherty) was born in 1851 in St. Louis, Missouri, to a French mother and Irish father. At the age of 19 she married a Creole, Oscar Chopin, and moved to New Orleans where she stayed until her husband's death in 1883. She then moved back to her native town and began her career as a writer. Nearly all her stories are set in Louisiana with its multiethnic community of Creoles, Cajuns and Afro-Americans.

Her first two collections of short stories: *Bayou Folk* (1894) and *A Night in Acadie* (1897) met with some success. Her only novel, *The Awakening* (1899), although highly acclaimed in recent years, was rejected by her contemporaries. Her frank portrayal of a woman capable of leaving husband and children in her search for self-assertion and sexual freedom was unacceptable to a late 19th century audience. This condemnation of her work on purely moralistic grounds had a very negative effect on her writing and she was to publish no more books after *The Awakening*. When she died in 1904 she had been almost completely forgotten as a writer.

Before reading

1 What does the word 'Louisiana' suggest to you? Write your ideas on the spidergram below.

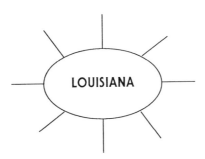

2 What do you know about the southern counties of the United States during the 19th century?

3 Look at the following words taken from the story. What do they suggest to you?
- Madame
- Monsieur
- plantation
- slaves

4 What do you expect the story to be about?

5 Listen to the first part of the story and complete the family tree on page 91.

AS THE DAY was pleasant, Madame Valmondé drove over to L'Abri to see Désirée and the baby.

It made her laugh to think of Désirée with a baby. Why, it seemed but yesterday that Désirée was little more than
5 a baby herself; when Monsieur in riding through the gateway of Valmondé had found her lying asleep in the shadow of the big stone pillar. [1]

The little one awoke in his arms and began to cry for "Dada." That was as much as she could do or say. Some people thought she might have strayed there of her own accord, for she was of the toddling age. [2] The
10 prevailing belief was that she had been purposely left by a party of Texans, whose canvas-covered wagon, [3] late in the day, had crossed the ferry that Coton Maïs kept, just below the plantation. In time Madame Valmondé abandoned every speculation but the one that Désirée had been sent to her by a beneficent Providence to be the child of her affection,
15 seeing that she was without child of the flesh. For the girl grew to be beautiful and gentle, affectionate and sincere, – the idol of Valmondé.

It was no wonder, when she stood one day against the stone pillar in whose shadow she had lain asleep, eighteen years before, that Armand Aubigny riding by and seeing her there, had fallen in love with her. That
20 was the way all the Aubignys fell in love, as if struck [4] by a pistol shot. The wonder was that he had not loved her before; for he had known her since his father brought him home from Paris, a boy of eight, after his mother died there. The passion that awoke in him that day, when he saw her at the gate, swept along [5] like an avalanche, [6] or like a prairie [7] fire, or
25 like anything that drives headlong [8] over all obstacles.

---

1   **pillar** ['pɪlə] : column of stone.

2   **of the toddling age** : of the age when children have just learnt to walk.

3   **canvas-covered wagon** ['wægən] : vehicle covered with a strong cloth typical of the Far West.

4   **struck** : hit.

5   **swept along** : moved out of control.

6   **avalanche** ['ævəlɑːntʃ] : mass of snow that slides down the side of a mountain.

7   **prairie** ['preəri] : wide, grassy area typical of North America.

8   **headlong** : without stopping.

Désirée's Baby

Monsieur Valmondé grew practical and wanted things well considered: that is, the girl's obscure origin. Armand looked into her eyes and did not care. He was reminded that she was nameless. What did it matter about a name when he could give her one of the oldest and proudest in Louisiana? He ordered the *corbeille* [9] from Paris, and contained himself with what patience he could until it arrived; then they were married.

30

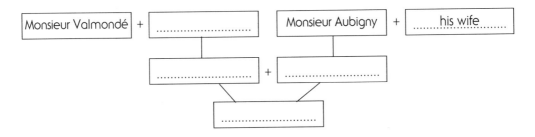

Now listen to this section again and answer the question below:

- What is unusual about Désirée?

6 In the table below write down what you have learnt about Désirée and Armand from the first part of the story.

DÉSIRÉE	
ARMAND	

7 Read the next section and make notes in the table on page 94.

9   *corbeille* : (French) presents from a fiancée to his betrothed.

Madame Valmondé had not seen Désirée and the baby for four weeks. When she reached L'Abri she shuddered [10] at the first sight of it, as she
35 always did. It was a sad looking place, which for many years had not known the gentle presence of a mistress, old Monsieur Aubigny having married and buried his wife in France, and she having loved her own land too well ever to leave it. The roof came down steep and black like a cowl, [11] reaching out beyond the wide galleries that encircled the yellow
40 stuccoed house. Big, solemn oaks grew close to it, and their thick-leaved, far-reaching [12] branches shadowed it like a pall. [13] Young Aubigny's rule was a strict one, too, and under it his negroes had forgotten how to be gay, as they had been during the old master's easy-going and indulgent lifetime.

45 The young mother was recovering slowly, and lay full length, in her soft white muslins [14] and laces, [15] upon a couch. [16] The baby was beside her, upon her arm, where he had fallen asleep, at her breast. The yellow nurse woman sat beside a window fanning herself.

Madame Valmondé bent her portly [17] figure over Désirée and kissed
50 her, holding her an instant tenderly in her arms. Then she turned to the child.

"This is not the baby!" she exclaimed, in startled [18] tones. French was the language spoken at Valmondé in those days.

"I knew you would be astonished," laughed Désirée, "at the way he
55 has grown. The little *cochon de lait*! [19] Look at his legs, mamma, and his hands and finger-nails, – real finger-nails. Zandrine had to cut them this morning. Isn't it true, Zandrine?"

10   **shuddered** ['ʃʌdəd] : shook (with fear and repulsion).
11   **cowl** : large hood (as on a monk's habit).
12   **far-reaching** : long.
13   **pall** [pɔːl] : funeral cloth spread over a coffin.
14   **muslins** ['mʌzlɪnz] : clothes made from a light, fine cotton.
15   **laces** : delicate fabric with an ornamental design.
16   **couch** [kaʊtʃ] : long seat, like a bed.
17   **portly** : (fml) fat.
18   **startled** ['stɑːtəld] : surprised, astonished.
19   *cochon de lait* : (French) young piglet.

The woman bowed her turbaned head majestically, *"Mais si, Madame."*

"And the way he cries," went on Désirée, "is deafening. Armand heard him the other day as far away as La Blanche's cabin." 60

Madame Valmondé had never removed her eyes from the child. She lifted it and walked with it over to the window that was lightest. She scanned the baby narrowly, then looked as searchingly [20] at Zandrine, whose face was turned to gaze across the fields.

"Yes, the child has grown, has changed," said Madame Valmondé, 65 slowly, as she replaced it beside its mother. "What does Armand say?"

Désirée's face became suffused with a glow [21] that was happiness itself.

"Oh, Armand is the proudest father in the parish, I believe, chiefly because it is a boy, to bear his name; though he says not, – that he would 70 have loved a girl as well. But I know it isn't true. I know he says that to please me. And mamma," she added, drawing Madame Valmondé's head down to her and speaking in a whisper, "he hasn't punished one of them – not one of them – since baby is born. Even Negrillon, who pretended to have burnt his leg that he might rest [22] from work – he only laughed, and 75 said Negrillon was a great scamp. [23] Oh, mamma, I'm so happy; it frightens me."

What Désirée said was true. Marriage, and later the birth of his son had softened Armand Aubigny's imperious and exacting [24] nature greatly. This was what made the gentle Désirée so happy for she loved 80 him desperately. When he frowned [25] she trembled, but loved him. When he smiled, she asked no greater blessing of God. But Armand's dark, handsome face had not often been disfigured by frowns since the day he fell in love with her.

---

20   **searchingly** ['sɜːtʃɪŋli] : in a penetrating way.

21   **glow** [gləʊ] : warm expression.

22   **rest** : stay away.

23   **scamp** : rascal, bad boy.

24   **exacting** : demanding.

25   **frowned** [fraʊnd] : had a serious and worried expression.

a

MADAME VALMONDÉ'S REACTION TO THE PLACE

b

MADAME VALMONDÉ'S REACTION TO THE BABY

c

DETAILS OF ARMAND'S PERSONALITY

8 In the light of what you have read so far decide which of the adjectives given below you would choose to describe the following characters:

MONSIEUR VALMONDÉ	
MADAME VALMONDÉ	
DÉSIRÉE	
ARMAND	
OLD MONSIEUR AUBIGNY	

- cruel
- strict
- mild-mannered
- absent-minded
- passionate
- impulsive
- dependent

- single-minded
- generous
- sensitive
- detached
- submissive
- merciless
- prejudiced

- authoritarian
- open-minded
- charitable
- understanding
- liberal
- hard to please
- honest

9 How do you expect the story to develop? Discuss.

10 Listen to the next part of the story and answer the questions on page 98, tick the one you think is correct. Then read the text to check your answers.

85   When the baby was about three months old, Désirée awoke one day to the conviction that there was something in the air menacing her peace. It was at first too subtle to grasp. [26] It had only been a disquieting [27] suggestion; an air of mystery among the blacks; unexpected visits from far-off neighbours who could hardly account for their coming. Then a
90 strange, an awful change in her husband's manner, which she dared not ask him to explain. When he spoke to her, it was with averted [28] eyes, from which the old love-light seemed to have gone out. He absented himself from home; and when there, avoided her presence and that of her child, without excuse. And the very spirit of Satan seemed suddenly to
95 take hold of him in his dealings with [29] the slaves. Désirée was miserable enough to die.

    She sat in her room, one hot afternoon, in her *peignoir*, [30] listlessly drawing through her fingers the strands [31] of her long, silky brown hair that hung about her shoulders. The baby, half naked, lay asleep upon her
100 own great mahogany bed, that was like a sumptuous throne, with its satin-lined half-canopy. [32] One of La Blanche's little quadroon [33] boys –

---

26   **grasp** [grɑːsp] : (here) understand.
27   **disquieting** [dɪsˈkwaɪətɪŋ] : disturbing, worrying.
28   **averted** : (fml) turned away.
29   **dealings with** : (here) behaviour towards, treatment of.
30   *peignoir* : (French) dressing gown.
31   **strands** : locks of hair.
32   **half-canopy** : half cover over a bed.
33   **quadroon** : (rare) a person, one of whose four grandparents was black.

half naked too – stood fanning [34] the child slowly with a fan of peacock [35] feathers. Désirée's eyes had been fixed absently and sadly upon the baby, while she was striving to penetrate the threatening mist [36] that she felt closing about her. She looked from her child to the boy who stood beside 105 him, and back again; over and over. "Ah!" It was a cry that she could not help; which she was not conscious of having uttered. The blood turned like ice in her veins, and a clammy [37] moisture [38] gathered upon her face.

She tried to speak to the little quadroon boy; but no sound would come, at first. When he heard his name uttered, he looked up, and his 110 mistress was pointing to the door. He laid aside the great, soft fan, and obediently stole away, [39] over the polished floor, on his bare [40] tiptoes.

She stayed motionless, with gaze riveted [41] upon her child, and her face the picture of fright. [42]

Presently her husband entered the room, and without noticing her, 115 went to a table and began to search among some papers which covered it.

"Armand," she called to him, in a voice which must have stabbed [43] him, if he was human. But he did not notice. "Armand," she said again. Then she rose and tottered towards him. "Armand," she panted once more, clutching [44] his arm, "look at our child. What does it mean? tell 120 me."

He coldly but gently loosened her fingers from about his arm and thrust the hand away from him. "Tell me what it means!" she cried despairingly.

34   **fanning** : ventilating.

35   **peacock** ['piːkɒk] : large bird remarkable for its long colourful feathers.

36   **mist** : thin fog.

37   **clammy** : unpleasantly sticky.

38   **moisture** ['mɔɪstʃə] : (here) sweat.

39   **stole away** : went away quietly.

40   **bare** [beə] : naked.

41   **riveted** ['rɪvɪtɪd] : (here) fixed.

42   **fright** [fraɪt] : fear, horror.

43   **stabbed** : wounded (with a dagger).

44   **clutching** ['klʌtʃɪŋ] : holding tightly.

125 "It means," he answered lightly, "that the child is not white; it means that you are not white."

A quick conception [45] of all that this accusation meant for her nerved her [46] with unwonted [47] courage to deny it. "It is a lie; it is not true, I am white! Look at my hair, it is brown; and my eyes are gray, Armand, you

130 know they are gray. And my skin is fair," seizing his wrist. "Look at my hand; whiter than yours, Armand," she laughed hysterically.

"As white as La Blanche's," he returned cruelly; and went away leaving her alone with their child.

a What does Désirée notice about her husband's manner?

☐ a great tenderness

☐ a manifest joy

☐ a terrible change

b How does she feel?

☐ quite well

☐ unhappy

☐ happy

c Why does she utter a cry?

☐ because she suddenly realizes something

☐ because she feels ill

☐ because the baby is ill

45   **conception** : (here) realization.

46   **nerved** [nɜːvd] **her** : gave courage and determination.

47   **unwonted** : (fml) unusual, unexpected.

11 Now complete the following notes in your own words to explain what has happened.

When the baby was about three months old, Armand's manner

changed: ....

Désirée realized that there was something strange going on but couldn't say what it was until one day, while looking at the little quadroon boy fanning the baby, Désirée had a sudden painful

realization..

....

12 In this part of the story the atmosphere is increasingly threatening. Underline the words or phrases in the text which help to create this tension. Has the author used any metaphor which is particularly effective in conveying this idea?

13 Have your impressions of Armand and Désirée changed? Update the character chart in Activity 8 using the adjectives provided or make your own suggestions.

14 Think about how the story might develop.

a What do you think Armand will do?

....

b What will happen to Désirée?

....

As you read the last section of the story do the Activity on page 102.

When she could hold a pen in her hand, she sent a despairing letter to
135 Madame Valmondé.

"My mother, they tell me I am not white. Armand has told me I am
not white. For God's sake tell them it is not true. You must know it is not
true. I shall die. I must die. I cannot be so unhappy, and live."

The answer that came was as brief:

140 "My own Désirée: Come home to Valmondé; back to your mother who
loves you. Come with your child."

When the letter reached Désirée she went with it to her husband's
study, and laid it open upon the desk before which he sat. She was like a
stone image: silent, white, motionless after she placed it there.

145 In silence he ran his cold eyes over the written words. He said
nothing. "Shall I go, Armand?" she asked in tones sharp with agonized [48]
suspense.

"Yes, go."

"Do you want me to go?"

150 "Yes, I want you to go."

He thought Almighty God had dealt cruelly and unjustly with him;
and felt, somehow, that he was paying Him back in kind when he
stabbed thus into his wife's soul. Moreover he no longer loved her,
because of the unconscious injury [49] she had brought upon his home and
155 his name.

She turned away like one stunned [50] by a blow, and walked slowly
towards the door, hoping he would call her back.

"Good-by, Armand," she moaned.

He did not answer her. That was his last blow at fate.

160 Désirée went in search of her child. Zandrine was pacing the sombre [51]
gallery with it. She took the little one from the nurse's arms with no word
of explanation, and descending the steps, walked away, under the live-
oak branches.

---

48 **agonized** ['ægənaɪzd] : terrified.

49 **injury** : (here) offence.

50 **stunned** ['stʌnd] : shocked.

51 **sombre** : (fml) dark and oppressive.

It was an October afternoon; the sun was just sinking. [52] Out in the still
fields the negroes were picking cotton.   165

Désirée had not changed the thin white garment [53] nor the slippers
which she wore. Her hair was uncovered and the sun's rays brought a
golden gleam from its brown meshes. She did not take the broad, beaten
road which led to the far-off plantation of Valmondé. She walked across a
deserted field, where the stubble bruised [54] her tender feet, so delicately   170
shod, and tore her thin gown to shreds. [55]

She disappeared among the reeds and willows that grew thick along
the banks of the deep, sluggish [56] bayou; [57] and she did not come back
again.

Some weeks later there was a curious scene enacted [58] at L'Abri. In the   175
centre of the smoothly swept back yard was a great bonfire. Armand
Aubigny sat in the wide hallway that commanded a view of the spectacle;
and it was he who dealt out to a half dozen negroes the material which
kept this fire ablaze. [59]

A graceful cradle [60] of willow, with all its dainty [61] furbishings, [62] was   180
laid upon the pyre, which had already been fed with the richness of a
priceless *layette*. [63] Then there were silk gowns, and velvet and satin ones
added to these; laces, too, and embroideries; bonnets and gloves; for the
corbeille had been of rare quality.

The last thing to go was a tiny bundle [64] of letters; innocent little   185

---

52   **sinking** : going down.

53   **garment** : (fml) dress.

54   **bruised** [bru:zd] : injured.

55   **shreds** : small pieces.

56   **sluggish** : slow-moving.

57   **bayou** ['baɪu:] : (in the southern USA) marshy part of a river.

58   **enacted** : acted out.

59   **ablaze** : (fml) burning.

60   **cradle** ['kreɪdl] : small bed for a baby.

61   **dainty** : delicate and elegant.

62   **furbishings** : cushions, sheets, drapery.

63   *layette* : (French) set of clothes and other articles for a new-born baby.

64   **bundle** [bʌndl] : pile (tied together).

scribblings [65] that Désirée had sent to him during the days of their espousal. There was the remnant of one back in the drawer from which he took them. But it was not Désirée's; it was part of an old letter from his mother to his father. He read it. She was thanking God for the blessing of her husband's love: –

190

"But, above all," she wrote, "night and day, I thank the good God for having so arranged our lives that our dear Armand will never know that his mother, who adores him, belongs to the race that is cursed [66] with the brand of slavery."

15 Read the following statements given in scrambled order. Three of them contain incorrect information, find them and cross them out, then put the remaining five into the correct order.

- ☐ **a** Désirée sent a letter to her mother in which she asked to be told the truth about her origins.

- ☐ **b** Armand, who was still very much in love with his wife, reacted sympathetically and quickly forget about the problem.

- ☐ **c** Whilst looking through some old letters Armand learnt the truth about Désirée's origins.

- ☐ **d** Some weeks later Armand burnt everything that had belonged to Désirée and the baby.

- ☐ **e** In her letter Madame Valmondé told Désirée to come back to Valmondé.

- ☐ **f** When she asked Armand what he wanted her to do, he ordered her to leave.

- ☐ **g** She took the main road to Valmondé.

- ☐ **h** One October afternoon, Désirée took the baby and walked away from her home.

65   **scribblings** : quickly and carelessly written letters.

66   **cursed** : damned.

Now reconsider the story as a whole.

16 a   By contrasting Désirée's and Armand's positions you will see how
the narrator "tricks" the reader. Use your own words to complete
the notes below. Add any explanations you feel necessary (as in
the example).

> I   Désirée is a foundling   her origins are uncertain
> ....
>
> II   Armand's family is ....
>
> III   Armand spent his childhood in ....
>
> IV   His attitude to .... is harsh and unfair.

b   A frequent characteristic of stories of suspense and surprise is that
details which at first appear irrelevant in fact turn out to be of great
importance and may prepare the reader for the final outcome.
Consider for example: "Armand's dark, handsome face ..." (what
does the word "dark" suggest here?) or "like a pall" (suggesting
death). Can you find more examples of this technique in the text?

17   Choice of lexis is essential in creating certain impressions. Skim parts
2,3,4 and underline all the words and expressions which suggest
wealth and prosperity. What effect does this produce (think about the
difference between the world of the slaves and Désirée's world).

Now study the language (verbs, adjectives, images etc.) associated
with Désirée. Is it mostly static or dynamic? What effect does this type
of language produce?

Look at the statements below. Do you agree with them?

- The great emphasis given to Désirée's social status helps to
  emphasize her loneliness and isolation. Chopin is stressing the
  enormous distance between two worlds: the world of the rich and
  the world of slaves.

- Chopin makes the ending more effective by first highlighting the
  gap between two worlds and then suggesting that such a gap, in
  the person of Armand, doesn't exist.

- Désirée's world is essentially static and Désirée herself, in spite of
  her queen-like condition, is made to appear mostly passive.

18 Complete the following notes about Désirée with information from the text and say if you agree with what is written below. If not re-write these notes to express your own ideas.

Désirée is the subservient wife who shows all that is expected of her: respect, obedience, love and even reverence towards her husband. There is however a point in the narrative where the emotional dependence on her husband stressed by parallel sentences like (skim the end of Part 2) ....
...., is strongly questioned. Facing a reality which comes as a shock to her, she summons all the energy she is capable of and facing Armand with unmatched courage and extraordinary force bears herself to say (skim the end of Part 3) ....
.... In a way her disappearance is symbolic of a desire for regeneration. When she walks away in her thin, white garment without any worldly belongings, she has little of the woman and more of the "saint" ready to face her inevitable self-sacrifice. Perhaps the author intended her disappearance to be a symbolic death...

19 How would you define the language in "Désirée's Baby"?

- simple
- concise
- literary

- rich
- critical
- objective

- realistic
- refined
- other

20 In order to be able to decide on the type of narrator in this story it may be useful to analyse the way in which characters are presented, through whose eyes the setting is seen, etc. Decide whether the characters are presented from the narrator's or another character's point of view. Then answer the questions below.

	NARRATOR'S POINT OF VIEW	CHARACTER'S POINT OF VIEW
Désirée		
Armand		
Madame Valmondé		
Setting		

Does the narrator provide any commentary on characters and situations? Does the narrator interpret the characters' motives? What conclusions can you reach?

21 a Analyse the structure of the story. Put each of the following sentences given in scrambled order next to the correct heading. Put an arrow next to the sentence(s) where the flashback(s) occur.

1. Armand burns Désirée's and the baby's personal belongings.

2. Armand holds Désirée responsible for the baby's colour, a charge which she categorically denies, however, she understands that she has no choice but to go away.

3. Armand learns the truth about his origins from an old letter he comes across while searching through Désirée's things.

4. Désirée disappears with the baby.

5. On her journey to visit Désirée and the baby, Madame Valmondé recalls her daughter's childhood.

6. It becomes apparent that Désirée's baby is "not white".

BEGINNING ☐

MAIN EVENT ☐

CONSEQUENCES ☐

EVENT ☐

CONSEQUENCES ☐

CONCLUSION ☐

b Where is the main climax in the story?

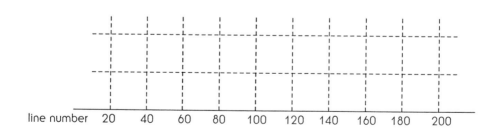

line number 20   40   60   80   100   120   140   160   180   200

22 Think about the title of the story. To what extent is the baby central to the story? Discuss.

23 What themes can you identify in this story? Which of the following seem to best illustrate the author's intended "message" in this story? Back up your answers with examples from the text.

- the conflict between the individual and society
- prejudice and race distinctions
- the contrast between appearance and reality
- the relationship between the sexes
- unhappy love
- male superiority / female dependence

Beyond the text

Activity

Work in pairs or groups and write a different ending for the story.

Talking points

1 Racial discrimination is just one aspect of discrimination. Can you think of any other examples of discrimination?

2 Read the following letter, originally printed in a national newspaper where a young black man describes how he was the victim of racial discrimination. While reading, answer the following questions:

- What made the police suspicious?
- How does Steve feel about the episode? Why?

Alister Morgan finds a heated reaction from young blacks in London

'We're all considered suspects'

Steve Campbell, 24, is a civil servant and lives in Wandsworth.

'One time I had gone to my sister's house because she has Sky Sports and I wanted to watch the basketball. Her video was busted [1] so I brought one from my house. I knew that I would look a bit strange walking down the street with a video under my arm so I put it in a sports bag.

The game finished about 2am and I started the three minute walk back to my house. The next thing I knew, a car screeched up [2] alongside me and two policemen jumped out and asked me what was in the bag. I knew that they had stopped me because I'm a single black male out in the street late at night but I didn't say anything. For

the next 15 minutes, I tried to convince them that the video belonged to me. I gave them a lot of minute [3] details about the video to prove it was mine, but they wouldn't listen. They were trying to get me to take them to where I lived. I didn't want to get busted [4] but I didn't want to take them home because it was the middle of the night and my family would not appreciate being woken up. I told them my address and showed them my house but

they insisted, and we ended up going inside the house and waking up my entire family.

This crackdown [5] will legitimise stopping black people. The majority of black people already think they get stopped more than whites. When it used to happen you at least felt that you were the victim of racism. Now, it seems, policemen have been given a licence – almost an order – to stop young blacks because now we're all being considered suspect.

As someone who considers himself British, I'm dismayed [6] that colour is still an issue. I was brought up in England but as soon as any trouble happens I stop being British and become black.'

(from *THE INDEPENDENT*)

---

1 **busted** : (infml) (here) broken, not working.

2 **screeched** : made a high, loud unpleasant noise (typical of wheels).

3 **minute** [maɪ'njuːt] : very careful and exact.

4 **busted** : (sl.) arrested.

5 **This crackdown** : These severe measures.

6 **dismayed** [dɪs'meɪd] : shocked and discouraged.

THE STORY OF AN HOUR

by KATE CHOPIN

Before reading

1 Have you ever sent or received a telegram? On which occasions are telegrams usually sent? Write your ideas on the spidergram below.

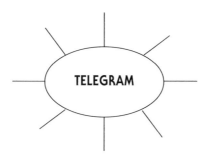

2 Look at the words below, then in pairs discuss what you think a story containing these words (with Mrs Mallard as the protagonist) will be about.

   • telegram

   • heart trouble

   • railroad disaster

   • Mr Mallard

3 The way people react to tragic events can vary according to their character or their cultural background. How do you think most people would react on hearing of a relative's death?

4 While reading the first part of the story focus on the underlined words, try to guess their meaning from the context and then match them with the definitions given below.

   • information

   • indirect suggestions

   • great number of birds

   • a look of careful consideration

   • great sorrow

   • empty, fixed look

   • discontinuous speech

   • extreme tiredness

K NOWING that Mrs Mallard was afflicted with a heart trouble, great care was taken to break [1] to her as gently as possible the news of her husband's death.

It was her sister Josephine who told her, in broken sentences; veiled hints that revealed in half concealing. [2] Her husband's friend Richards was there, too, near her. It was he who had been in the newspaper office when intelligence of the railroad [3] disaster was received, with Brently Mallard's name leading the list of "killed." He had only taken the time to assure himself of its truth by a second telegram, and had hastened [4] to forestall [5] any less careful, [6] less tender friend in bearing the sad message.

She did not hear the story as many women have heard the same, with a paralyzed inability to accept its significance. She wept at once, with sudden, wild [7] abandonment, in her sister's arms. When the storm of grief had spent itself she went away to her room alone. She would have no one follow her.

There stood, facing the open window, a comfortable, roomy armchair. Into this she sank, pressed down [8] by a physical exhaustion that haunted [9] her body and seemed to reach into her soul.

She could see in the open square before her house the tops of trees that were all aquiver [10] with the new spring life. The delicious breath of rain

1   **break** : give.

2   **concealing** : hiding.

3   **railroad** : (AmE) railways.

4   **hastened** : hurried.

5   **forestall** : (here) prevent.

6   **careful** : (here) sensitive.

7   **wild** : (here) uncontrolled, violent.

8   **pressed down** : weighted down.

9   **haunted** : obsessed.

10   **aquiver** : (fml) trembling.

was in the air. In the street below a peddler [11] was crying his wares. [12] The notes of a distant song which some one was singing reached her faintly, and <u>countless</u> <u>sparrows</u> were twittering in the eaves. [13]

There were patches [14] of blue sky showing here and there through the clouds that had met and piled [15] one above the other in the west facing her window.

She sat with her head thrown back [16] upon the cushion of the chair, quite motionless, except when a sob came up into her throat and shook her, as a child who has cried itself to sleep [17] continues to sob in its dreams.

She was young, with a fair, calm face, whose lines bespoke repression and even a certain strength. But now there was a <u>dull</u> <u>stare</u> in her eyes, whose gaze [18] was fixed away off yonder [19] on one of those patches of blue sky. It was not a <u>glance</u> <u>of</u> <u>reflection</u>, but rather indicated a suspension of intelligent thought.

11   **peddler** : street-seller.

12   **wares** [weəz] : goods, articles.

13   **eaves** [iːvz] : lower parts of roofs (where birds make nests).

14   **patches** : small areas.

15   **piled** : placed.

16   **thrown** [θrəʊn] **back** : resting.

17   **cried itself to sleep** : exhausted itself through crying until it fell asleep.

18   **gaze** : long steady look.

19   **off yonder** : (fml) over there.

5 What do we learn about the characters (appearance, psychological details, ...) and their relationship to each other? Fill in the table with examples from the text. Then discuss your answers in pairs.

Mrs Mallard	
Brently Mallard	
Josephine	
Richards	

SITUATION

- What has happened to Mr Mallard?

- How does Mrs Mallard react? Use your own words together with examples from the text to describe her reaction.

6 What have we learnt so far about Mr and Mrs Mallard's relationship? Discuss in pairs and give reasons for your answers. You may use the words below or add your own.

- happy marriage
- mutual love
- reciprocal respect
- a one-sided relationship
- routine existence
- miserable life

7 How do you think the story will develop? Will something unexpected happen or will one of the protagonists change in some way? Discuss. Listen to the next section to see whether your predictions were correct.

There was something coming to her and she was waiting for it, fearfully. What was it? She did not know; it was too subtle [20] and elusive to name. But she felt it, creeping [21] out of the sky, reaching toward her through the sounds, the scents, [22] the color that filled the air.

Now her bosom rose [23] and fell tumultuously. She was beginning to recognize this thing that was approaching to possess her, and she was striving [24] to beat it back with her will – as powerless as her two white slender [25] hands would have been.

When she abandoned herself a little whispered [26] word escaped her slightly parted [27] lips. She said it over and over under her breath: "free, free, free!" The vacant [28] stare and the look of terror that had followed it went from her eyes. They stayed keen [29] and bright. Her pulses [30] beat fast, and the coursing [31] blood warmed and relaxed every inch of her body.

She did not stop to ask if it were or were not a monstrous joy that held her. A clear and exalted perception enabled her to dismiss [32] the suggestion as trivial. [33]

40

45

50

20   **subtle** : (here) difficult to understand.
21   **creeping** : moving slowly.
22   **scents** [sɛnts] : perfumes, smells.
23   **rose** : went up and down.
24   **striving** : trying very hard.
25   **slender** : thin.
26   **whispered** ['wɪspəd] : spoken softly.
27   **slightly parted** ['slaɪtli paːtɪd] : just a little opened.
28   **vacant** : (here) absent.
29   **keen** : sharp.
30   **pulses** : regular beatings of blood round the body.
31   **coursing** : flowing rapidly.
32   **dismiss** : send away.
33   **trivial** : unimportant, insignificant.

8 The section you have just heard explores Mrs Mallard's emotional world. Look back at the text and complete the table. Use the third column for your deductions if any.

WHAT HAPPENS	CHARACTER'S REACTIONS	WHAT YOU INFER
There was something coming to her	She was waiting for it fearfully	

Can you draw any conclusions from this?

What does the interplay between human and non-human suggest to you? Focus on the lines given below and try to explain what kind of experience Mrs Mallard has had.

"Now her bosom rose and fell tumultuously. She was beginning to recognize this thing which was approaching to possess her [...] When she abandoned herself a little whispered word escaped her slightly parted lips [...] Her pulses beat fast, and the coursing blood warmed and relaxed every inch of her body".

What is the resulting image here?

9 Read the next part and make notes on Mrs Mallard's thoughts about the future, the past and the present. Fill in the boxes to analyse the progression of her thoughts and feelings.

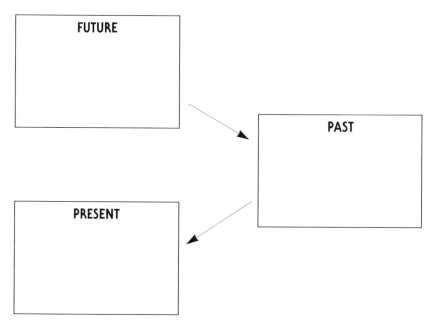

She knew that she would weep again when she saw the kind, tender hands folded [34] in death; the face that had never looked save with love upon her, fixed and gray and dead. But she saw beyond that bitter moment a long procession of years to come that would belong to her absolutely. And she opened and spread her arms out [35] to them in welcome.

There would be no one to live for her during those coming years; she would live for herself. There would be no powerful [36] will bending [37]

34   **folded** : crossed over his chest.
35   **spread her arms out** : opened out her arms.
36   **powerful** : very strong.
37   **bending** : forcing (in a particular direction).

hers in that blind persistence [38] with which men and women believe they have a right to impose a private [39] will upon a fellow-creature. A kind intention [40] or a cruel intention made the act seem no less a crime as she

65   looked upon it in that brief moment of illumination.

And yet she had loved him – sometimes. Often she had not. What did it matter! What could love, the unsolved mystery, count for [41] in face of this possession of self-assertion [42] which she suddenly recognized as the strongest impulse of her being!

70   "Free! Body and soul free!" she kept whispering.

Josephine was kneeling [43] before the closed door with her lips to the keyhole, imploring for admission. "Louise, open the door! I beg; open the door – you will make yourself ill. What are you doing, Louise? For heaven's sake open the door."

75   "Go away. I am not making myself ill." No; she was drinking in a very elixir of life through that open window.

10 Look back at Activity 6. Have your ideas about the relationship between Mr and Mrs Mallard changed?

---

38   **persistence** : firmness, tenacity.

39   **private** : (here) personal.

40   **intention** : purpose.

41   **count for** : mean, signify.

42   **self-assertion** : forceful affirmation of her personality.

43   **kneeling** ['niːlɪŋ] : with her knees on the floor.

11 Which adjectives would you use to describe Mr and Mrs Mallard? Choose from the list below and fill in the table. Be prepared to give reasons for your choice!

- repressed
- single-minded
- open-minded
- loving
- domineering
- passionate
- cold
- formal
- submissive
- restrained
- rational
- sensitive
- affectionate
- over-protective
- insecure
- indifferent

MRS MALLARD	
MR MALLARD	

12 A sense of exhilaration as well as the concepts of freedom and self-fulfilment are further developed in this part of the story. Find and underline examples of them in the text.

13 What do you think will happen next in the story? Discuss your ideas in pairs, then write down a few notes outlining your predictions. Listen to the next section of the story.

Her fancy was running riot [44] along those days ahead of her. Spring days, and summer days, and all sorts of days that would be her own. She breathed [45] a quick prayer that life might be long. It was only yesterday
80 she had thought with a shudder [46] that life might be long.

She arose at length and opened the door to her sister's importunities. [47] There was a feverish triumph in her eyes, and she carried herself [48] unwittingly [49] like a goddess of Victory. She clasped her sister's waist, and together they descended the stairs. Richards stood waiting for them
85 at the bottom.

Some one was opening the front door with a latchkey. [50] It was Brently Mallard who entered, a little travel-stained; [51] composedly carrying his grip-sack [52] and umbrella. He had been far from the scene of accident, and did not even know there had been one. He stood amazed at
90 Josephine's piercing [53] cry; at Richards' quick motion to screen him [54] from the view of his wife.

Bu Richards was too late.

When the doctors came they said she had died of heart disease – of joy that kills.

Were your predictions right? Were you surprised by the ending?

44 **riot** ['raɪət] : free, without control.
45 **breathed** [briːθd] : said softly.
46 **shudder** : (here) tremble because of fear.
47 **importunities** : insistent requests.
48 **carried herself** : moved.
49 **unwittingly** [ʌn'wɪtɪŋli] : unconsciously.
50 **latchkey** ['lætʃkiː] : key of the front door.
51 **travel-stained** : dirtied because of his long travel.
52 **grip-sack** : (AmE) bag.
53 **piercing** : (here) very loud.
54 **screen him** : protect him.

Now reconsider the story as a whole.

14 Think about how setting and character are connected. In your opinion why is the setting so important? Choose among the possibilities given below:

- it makes the character's sorrow stand out more by effectively contrasting it to the positivity of nature;

- it suggests spiritual regeneration and anticipates the sense of fulfilment the character will experience soon after;

- it is a co-protagonist, thus essential to plot development;

- it illustrates Mrs Mallard's sensitiveness: she is the kind of person who can communicate with nature.

15 Examine the style in "The Story of an Hour". Read the list of possibilities given below: cross out those you don't agree with and find examples in the text for the others.

EXAMPLES

- There are a lot of dynamic (action) verbs

- Verbs of perception and emotion are widely used

- Some of the adjectives refer to states of mind

- There are more concrete than abstract nouns

- There are a few key words which acquire symbolic significance during the course of the story

- There is some figurative language

- The language is straightforward and "colourless"

- Greater emphasis is placed on the physical rather than the psychological in the presentation of the characters

How do you explain the writer's stylistic choices in relation to content? Do you find them appropriate?

16 How would you describe the language and style in "The Story of an Hour"? Choose from the adjectives below.

- literary
- neutral
- basic
- refined
- everyday
- emotional
- realistic

17 Study the function of the final scene. In a way it could be considered a sort of "coda", following Mrs Mallard's journey towards self-fulfilment and liberation, which can be said the core of the story. Read the list of alternatives given below and select the one(s) you agree with. The function of the final scene is:

- to create surprise
- to establish a sort of poetic "justice": Mrs. Mallard's just reward, because her husband's death caused her to feel exhalted and liberated, rather than grief
- to arouse irony
- to make Mrs Mallard's self-assertion more effective
- to provide a sort of criticism of society. The "liberated" woman cannot exist: she is doomed to fail
- to develop a pattern by reversing the roles

Think about the following: Mr Mallard's death = Mrs Mallard's life
Mr Mallard's life = Mrs Mallard's death

18 How would you define the general tone of the story?

- neutral
- serious
- ironic
- detached
- moralizing
- sarcastic
- biased
- other

19 Is the title effective? Do you think it should be interpreted literally, that is, could the events in the story have taken place in one hour? If you were to change the title, what would you suggest as an alternative?

20 What is the central theme to the story?

- unrequited love
- lack of love
- self-assertion and recognition
- the power of love
- spiritual liberation
- the price of freedom
- the clash between individual and society
- male oppression of women
- the restrictions imposed by society
- disappointment

Beyond the text

Activity 1

Now go beyond the story. Write a description of Mr Mallard's reaction to the tragedy of his wife's death. Choose either situation given below.

a   Mr Mallard has always been deeply in love with his wife and is terribly upset by her death.

b   Mr Mallard has been having an affair with another woman, who he is in love with but he has never been able to leave his devoted wife. Now destiny has decided for him.

Start like this:
He couldn't believe his eyes. His wife ....
....

Activity 2

Write a short comparison of "The Story of an Hour" and "Désirée's Baby", highlighting any common features you have found. Take into account theme, style, character development or any other aspect you may want to focus on. Use the language of comparison and contrast.

Here are some examples:

In many ways	On the contrary
To some extent	Compared with
In some respects	Unlike
Similarly	On the other hand
Likewise	While
In the same way	However

....

....

....

....

....

....

Talking points

1   One of Kate Chopin's major concerns at the time she was writing, was the condition of the woman.
    The struggle for equality between the sexes at the turn of the century can be seen in the suffragette movement which made significant achievements (the right to vote, employment in factories etc.) possible.
    How much do you know about the topic? Discuss.
    The 20th century has seen many changes in society including dramatic social and political progress in the position of women in society ... Yet, this gradual improvement in the equality between the sexes is as yet unfinished. Discuss.

2 Read the article below illustrating the position of women in Great Britain. Is the situation similar in your country? Discuss.

Today's woman is still struggling in a man's world

by CATHERINE MILTON, SOCIAL SERVICES CORRESPONDENT

WOMEN have loosened the shackles [1] of domestic drudgery [2] only to become weary drones [3] in the workplace, Government research suggests. *An Official Look at Ms Britain*, published yesterday, will infuriate die-hard [4] feminists and further confuse many of the nation's 24 million women, increasingly perplexed about how to lead fulfilling lives.

Last year, almost 45 per cent of Britain's paid workforce was female, compared with 37 per cent in 1971.

However, few women have managed to persuade men to share domestic responsabilities, leaving most doubly burdened: they are unable to compete properly at work and are too stressed to use their free time imaginatively.

While today's women are better educated and harder working, their jobs are still lowlier than men's and less well paid, according to the study compiled by the Central Statistical Office.

Women's career progress is slightly set back if they take time out to have children. More than five times as many women as men do some from of part-time work, particularly when they have children – a factor linked to slower progress at work. About half the population disapproves of women working when they have children, and 63 per cent believe women should work part-time when their children are at school.

Women have, however, been making progress in traditionally male occupatons. Britain's 20,000 women police officers make up 13 per cent of the force. The proportion of women sergeants doubled to 6 per cent in the ten years to 1994 while the proportion of women constables increased from 11 to 16 per cent.

About 30 per cent of practising solicitors in England and Wales last year were women,compared with 12 per cent ten years ago. There are more women than men among solicitors aged 30 and under.

Women are paid less than men on average: 33 per cent of women earn under £190 a week, compared with 13 per cent of men; 75 per cent of men earn £230 a week compared with 50 per cent of women.

Women are also likely to earn less than the men with whom they share their lives: only 13 per cent of couples report that the female half earn more than £50 per week more than the male.

Men and women are equally likely to train during their careers, but for different reason. Men want to improve their chances of promotion while women want to make their work more interesting.

(from THE TIMES)

---

1 **shackles** : metal rings linked by a chain, used for fastening a prisoner's wists (or ankles) together, (here) (figurative).

2 **drudgery** : hard boring work.

3 **drones** : (derog.) idlers, people who live on the work of others.

4 **diehard** : (here) convinced.

THE LOTTERY

by Shirley Jackson

SHIRLEY JACKSON was born in San Francisco in 1919 and spent most of her youth in California. A prolific writer, she was acclaimed by the critics when her extraordinary short story "The Lottery" appeared in *The New Yorker* in 1948. "The Lottery", like many of her short stories, was dramatized for radio and television.

Her works include collections of short stories: *Life among the Savages* (1953), *Raising Demons* (1957) and *Come Along with Me* (published posthumously in 1968) as well as a number of novels: *The Bird's Nest* (1954), *We Have Always Lived in the Castle* (1962) and many others.

Her novels typically include at least one violent death, and are permeated with an atmosphere of mystery and often deal with the supernatural.

She died in 1965 at the age of 46.

Before reading

1 Look at the title of this short story. What do you think the story will be about?

2 What is a lottery? What happens in a lottery?

3 How do people normally feel when they take part in a lottery? Choose from the adjectives below or add your own.

- excited
- curious
- indifferent
- bored
- cheerful
- nervous
- anxious
- hopeful

4 Read the first part of the story and fill in the table below taking your examples from the text (some have been done for you).

WHO	WHAT
Bobbie Martin	filled his pockets with stones
....	....
....	stood aside
....	....
....	spoke about their work, made quiet jokes
the women	....
....	....
....	....

SETTING	Time ....
	Place ....

T HE MORNING of June 27th was clear and sunny, with the fresh warmth of a full-summer day; the flowers were blossoming profusely, [1] and the grass was richly green. The people of the village began to gather in the square,

5 between the post office and the bank, around ten o'clock; in some towns there were so many people that the lottery took two days and had to be started on June 26th, but in this village, where there were only about three hundred people, the whole lottery took only about two hours, so it could begin at ten o'clock in the morning and still be through in time to

10 allow the villagers to get home for noon dinner.

The children assembled [2] first, of course. School was recently over for the summer, and the feeling of liberty sat uneasily [3] on most of them; they tended to gather together quietly for a while before they broke into boisterous [4] play, and their talk was still of the classroom and the teacher,

15 of books and reprimands. [5] Bobby Martin had already stuffed [6] his pockets full of stones, and the other boys soon followed his example, selecting the smoothest and roundest stones; Bobby and Harry Jones and Dickie Delacroix – the villagers pronounced the name "Dellacroy" – eventually made a great pile of stones in one corner of the square and

20 guarded it against the raids [7] of the other boys. The girls stood aside, talking among themselves, looking over their shoulders at the boys, and the very small children rolled in the dust or clung [8] to the hands of their older brothers or sisters.

Soon the men began to gather, surveying their own children, speaking

25 of planting and rain, tractors and taxes. They stood together, away from

---

1 **profusely** [prə'fjuːsli] : in abundance.

2 **assembled** : met together.

3 **uneasily** [ʌn'iːzɪli] : uncomfortably.

4 **boisterous** ['bɔɪstərəs] : lively and noisy.

5 **reprimands** : (here) when teachers or parents showed strong disapproval of their actions.

6 **stuffed** : (here) completely filled.

7 **raids** [reɪdz] : surprise attacks.

8 **clung** [klʌŋ] : held on.

the pile of stones in the corner, and their jokes were quiet, and they smiled rather than laughed. The women, wearing faded house dresses [9] and sweaters, came shortly after their menfolk. They greeted one another and exchanged bits of gossip as they went to join their husbands. Soon the women, standing by their husbands, began to call to their children, and the children came reluctantly, having to be called four or five times. Bobby Martin ducked under his mother's grasping hand [10] and ran, laughing, back to the pile of stones. His father spoke up sharply, and Bobby came quickly and took his place between his father and his oldest brother.

The lottery was conducted – as were the square dances, the teenage club, the Halloween program – by Mr Summers, who had time and energy to devote to civic activities. He was a round-faced, jovial [11] man, and he ran the coal business; and people were sorry for him, because he had no children and his wife was a scold. [12] When he arrived in the square, carrying the black wooden box, there was murmur [13] of conversation among the villagers, and he waved and called. "Little late today, folks." [14] The postmaster, Mr Graves, followed him, carrying a three-legged stool; [15] and the stool was put in the center of the square, and Mr Summers set the black box down on it. The villagers kept their distance, leaving a space between themselves and the stool, and when Mr Summers said, "Some of you fellows want to give me a hand?" there was a hesitation before two men, Mr Martin and his oldest son, Baxter, came forward to hold the box steady on the stool while Mr Summers stirred up [16] the papers inside it.

9   **faded house dresses** : dresses (worn as protection over everyday clothes) which have lost their colour.

10   **grasping hand** : hand which tried to hold him firmly.

11   **jovial** : merry, good-humoured.

12   **scold** [skəʊld] : (infml) woman who is discontented and easily angered.

13   **murmur** ['mɜːmə] : low, continuous sound.

14   **folks** : (infml) people.

15   **stool** [stuːl] : seat without back or armrests.

16   **stirred** ['stɜːd] **up** : mixed up.

5 Read the next part of the story. What do you learn about the box and the ritual surrounding the lottery? Make notes under the headings below.

BOX	
RITUAL	

The original paraphernalia [17] for the lottery had been lost long ago, and the black box now resting on the stool had been put into use even before Old Man Warner, the oldest man in town, was born. Mr Summers spoke frequently to the villagers about making a new box, but no one
55   liked to upset [18] even as much tradition as was represented by the black box. There was a story that the present box had been made with some pieces of the box that had preceded it, the one that had been constructed when the first people settled down to make a village here. Every year, after the lottery, Mr Summers began talking again about a new box, but
60   every year the subject was allowed to fade off [19] without anything being done. The black box grew shabbier [20] each year; by now it was no longer completely black but splintered badly along one side to show the original wood color, and in some places faded or stained.

Mr Martin and his oldest son, Baxter, held the black box securely on

---

17   **paraphernalia** [pærəfə'neɪlɪə] : equipment.
18   **upset** : disturb.
19   **fade off** : disappear, vanish.
20   **grew shabbier** ['ʃæbɪə] : was in increasingly bad condition.

the stool until Mr Summers had stirred the papers thoroughly with his 65
hand. Because so much of the ritual had been forgotten or discarded, Mr
Summers had been successful in having slips of paper substituted for the
chips of wood that had been used for generations. Chips [21] of wood, Mr
Summers had argued, had been all very well when the village was tiny,
but now that the population was more than three hundred and likely to 70
keep on growing, it was necessary to use something that would fit more
easily into the black box. The night before the lottery, Mr Summers and
Mr Graves made up the slips of paper and put them into the box, and it
was then taken to the safe of Mr Summers' coal company and locked up
until Mr Summers was ready to take it to the square next morning. The 75
rest of the year, the box was put away, sometimes one place, sometimes
another; it had spent one year in Mr Grave's barn [22] and another year
underfoot in the post office, and sometimes it was set on a shelf in the
Martin grocery and left there.

There was a great deal of fussing [23] to be done before Mr Summers 80
declared the lottery open. There were the lists to make up – of heads of
families, heads of households in each family, members of each household [24]
in each family. There was the proper swearing-in [25] of Mr Summers by
the postmaster, as the official of the lottery; at one time, some people
remembered, there had been a recital [26] of some sort, performed by the 85
official of the lottery, a perfunctory, [27] tuneless chant that had been
rattled off [28] duly each year; some people believed that the official of the
lottery used to stand just so when he said or sang it; others believed that
he was supposed to walk among the people; but years and years ago this

21   **Chips** : Small pieces.
22   **barn** : farm building for storing grain etc.
23   **fussing** ['fʌsɪŋ] : worrying about petty details.
24   **household** ['haushəuld] : the occupants of a house regarded as a unit.
25   **swearing-in** : inauguration into office by taking an oath.
26   **recital** [rɪ'saɪtl] : a public performance of something learned or prepared.
27   **perfunctory** [pə'fʌŋktəri] : (fml) nominal, mechanical.
28   **rattled off** : recited rapidly.

90 part of the ritual [29] had been allowed to lapse. There had been also a
ritual salute, which the official of the lottery had had to use in addressing
each person who came up to draw [30] from the box, but this also had
changed with time, until now it was felt necessary only for the official to
speak to each person approaching. Mr Summers was very good at all this;
95 in his clean white shirt and blue jeans, with one hand resting carelessly
on the black box he seemed very proper [31] and important as he talked
interminably to Mr Graves and the Martins.

6 Can you find references in the text which demonstrate how important
an event the lottery is in the villagers' lives? Have you noticed
anything strange about the lottery?

7 The points below summarize the next part of the story. Some of them,
however, do not describe the facts accurately.
Go through them carefully, read the next section and then decide which
of them are right and correct the ones that need to be changed.

a Mrs Hutchinson was almost late because she was busy doing her
housework and nearly forgot what day it was.

b Mr Summers makes sure that one representative from each family
is present. As a rule it is up to the head of the family to draw, but
in exceptional circumstances a wife or a grown boy are allowed to
draw.

c The crowd is noisy while Mr Summers is giving out instructions about
the lottery. He explains that heads of family will draw last and are
not to look at their piece of paper until everyone has had a turn.

d The validity of lotteries is strongly questioned by Old Man Warren.
However Mr Adams is a strong supporter of them, he says, "Lottery
in June, corn be heavy soon".

29   **ritual** : ceremony.
30   **draw** [drɔː] : take out.
31   **proper** : respectable.

Just as Mr Summers finally left off talking and turned to the assembled villagers, Mrs Hutchinson came hurriedly along the path to the square, her sweater thrown over her shoulders, and slid into place in the back of the crowd. "Clean [32] forgot what day it was," she said to Mrs Delacroix, who stood next to her, and they both laughed softly. "Thought my old man was out back stacking [33] wood," Mrs Hutchinson went on, "and then I looked out the window and the kids was gone, and then I remembered it was the twenty-seventh and came a-running." She dried her hands on her apron, [34] and Mrs Delacroix said, "You're in time, though. They're still talking away up there."

Mrs Hutchinson craned [35] her neck to see through the crowd and found her husband and children standing near the front. She tapped [36] Mrs Delacroix on the arm as a farewell and began to make her way through the crowd. The people separated good-humoredly to let her through; two or three people said, in voices just loud enough to be heard across the crowd, "Here comes your Mrs Hutchinson", and "Bill, she made it after all." Mrs Hutchinson reached her husband, and Mr Summers, who had been waiting, said cheerfully, "Thought we were going to have to get on without you, Tessie." Mrs Hutchinson said, grinning, [37] "Wouldn't have me leave m'dishes in the sink, now, would you Joe?" and soft laughter ran through the crowd as the people stirred back into position after Mrs Hutchinson's arrival.

"Well, now," Mr Summers said soberly, "guess we better get started, get this over with, so's [38] we can go back to work. Anybody ain't [39] here?"

"Dunbar," several people said. "Dunbar, Dunbar."

Mr Summers consulted his list. "Clyde Dunbar," he said. "That's right. He's broke his leg, hasn't he? Who's drawing for him?"

32   **Clean** : (here) Completely.
33   **stacking** : putting into a neat pile.
34   **apron** [eɪˈprən] : garment protecting a person's clothes (esp. while cooking).
35   **craned** [kreɪnd] : stretched out (in order to see).
36   **tapped** [tæpt] : hit gently with finger.
37   **grinning** : smiling broadly, showing teeth.
38   **so's** : (non-standard) so as.
39   **ain't** : (non-standard) (here) not.

125   "Me, I guess," a woman said, and Mr Summers turned to look at her. "Wife draws for her husband," Mr Summers said. "Don't you have a grown boy to do it for you, Janey?" Although Mr Summers and everyone else in the village knew the answer perfectly well, it was the business of the official of the lottery to ask such questions formally. Mr Summers
130   waited with an expression of polite interest while Mrs Dunbar answered.

    "Horace's not but sixteen yet," Mrs Dunbar said regretfully. "Guess I gotta [40] fill in for the old man this year."

    "Right," Mr Summers said. He made a note on the list he was holding. Then he asked, "Watson boy drawing this year?"

135   A tall boy in the crowd raised his hand, "Here," he said. "I'm drawing for m'mother and me." He blinked his eyes [41] nervously and ducked his head as several voices in the crowd said things like "Good fellow, Jack", and "Glad to see your mother's got a man to do it."

    "Well," Mr Summers said, "guess that's everyone. Old Man Warner
140   make it?"

    "Here," a voice said, and Mr Summers nodded.

    A sudden hush [42] fell on the crowd as Mr Summers cleared his throat and looked at the list. "All ready?" he called. "Now, I'll read the names – heads of families first – and the men come up and take a paper out of the
145   box. Keep the paper folded [43] in your hand without looking at it until everyone has had a turn. Everything clear?"

    The people had done it so many times that they only half listened to the directions; most of them were quiet, wetting their lips, not looking around. Then Mr Summers raised one hand high and said, "Adams." A
150   man disengaged [44] himself from the crowd and came forward. "Hi, Steve," Mr Summers said, and Mr Adams said, "Hi, Joe." The grinned at one another humorlessly and nervously. Then Mr Adams reached as he turned and went hastily back to his place in the crowd, where he stood a

---

40   **gotta** : (non-standard) have to.

41   **blinked his eyes** : shut and opened his eyes quickly.

42   **hush** [hʌʃ] : silence.

43   **folded** : bent, doubled.

44   **disengaged** : detached, separated.

little apart from his family, not looking down at his hand.

"Allen," Mr Summers said. "Anderson ... Bentham."   155

"Seems like there's no time at all between lotteries any more," Mrs Delacroix said to Mrs Graves in the back row. [45] "Seems like we got through with the last one only last week."

"Time sure goes fast," Mrs Graves said.

"Clark ... Delacroix."   160

"There goes my old man," Mrs Delacroix said. She held her breath while her husband went forward.

"Dunbar," Mr Summers said, and Mrs Dunbar went steadily to the box while one of the women said, "Go on, Janey," and another said, "There she goes."   165

"We're next," Mrs Graves said. She watched while Mr Graves came around from the side of the box, greeted Mr Summers gravely, and selected a slip of paper from the box. By now, all through the crowd there were men holding the small folded papers in their large hands, turning them over and over nervously. Mrs Dunbar and her two sons stood   170 together, Mrs Dunbar holding the slip of paper.

"Harburt ... Hutchinson."

"Get up there, Bill," Mrs Hutchinson said, and the people near her laughed.

"Jones."   175

"They do say," Mr Adams said to Old Man Warner, who stood next to him, "that over in the north village they're talking of giving up the lottery."

Old Man Warner snorted. [46] "Pack [47] of crazy fools," he said. "Listening to the young folks, nothing's good enough for *them*. Next   180 thing you know, they'll be wanting to go back to living in caves, nobody work any more, live *that* way for a while. Used to be a saying about 'Lottery in June, corn be heavy soon.' First thing you know, we'd all be

45   **row** [rəʊ] : line.

46   **snorted** : forced air out through the nose in an expression of contempt.

47   **Pack** : (here derog.) Group.

eating stewed [48] chickweed [49] and acorns. [50] There's *always* been a lottery,"
185   he added petulantly. "Bad enough to see young Joe Summers up there joking with everybody."

"Some places have already quit lotteries," Mrs Adams said.

"Nothing but trouble in *that*." Old Man Warner said stoutly. "Pack of young fools."

190   "Martin." And Bobby Martin watched his father go forward. "Overdyke ... Percy."

"I wish they'd hurry," Mrs Dunbar said to her older son. "I wish they'd hurry."

"They're almost through," her son said.

195   "You get ready to run tell Dad," Mrs Dunbar said.

Mr Summers called his own name and then stepped forward precisely and selected a slip from the box. Then he called, "Warner."

"Seventy-seventh year I been in the lottery," Old Man Warner said as he went through the crowd. "Seventy-seventh time."

200   "Watson." The tall boy came awkwardly [51] through the crowd. Someone said, "Don't be nervous, Jack," and Mr Summers said, "Take your time, son."

"Zanini."

---

8 a Scan the text you have read so far and focus on the general atmosphere. Think about the setting, the people's mood and details we are given about the box. Underline words and expressions which, in your opinion, contribute to create a particular atmosphere. Which of the words below do you think best describe it?

- exciting   • cheerful   • menacing   • pleasant
- positive   • sinister   • routine   • tense

---

48   **stewed** [stjuːd] : cooked slowly (in liquid).

49   **chickweed** : small-leaved plants.

50   **acorns** : fruits of the oak tree.

51   **awkwardly** ['ɔːkwədli] : in an embarassed way.

b In the light of your answer to the above question how do you think the villagers view the lottery? Think of the dispute between the Adams family and Old Man Warner.

9 How do you expect the story to develop?

10 In the next part of the story a "lottery within lottery" takes place. How do you expect it to work? (Consider that up to now only one representative of each family has drawn).

11 Read the next section and answer the questions on page 141.

After that, there was a long pause, a breathless pause; until Mr Summers, holding his slip of paper in the air, said, "All right, fellows." 205 For a minute, no one moved, and then all the slips of paper were opened. Suddenly, all the women began to speak at once, saying, "Who is it?" "Who's got it?" "Is it the Dunbars?" "Is it the Watsons?" Then the voices began to say, "It's Hutchinson. It's Bill." "Bill Hutchinson's got it."

"Go tell your father," Mrs Dunbar said to her older son. 210

People began to look around to see the Hutchinsons. Bill Hutchinson was standing quiet, staring down at the paper in his hand. Suddenly, Tessie Hutchinson show to Mr Summers, "You didn't give him time enough to take any paper he wanted. I saw you. It wasn't fair!"

"Be a good sport, Tessie," Mrs Delacroix called, and Mrs Graves said, 215 "All of us took the same chance."

"Shut up, Tessie," Bill Hutchinson said.

"Well, everyone," Mr Summers said, "that was done pretty fast, and now we got to be hurrying a little more to get done in time." He consulted his next list. "Bill," he said, "you draw for the Hutchinson family. You 220 got any other household in the Hutchinsons?"

"There's Don and Eva," Mrs Hutchinson yelled. [52] "Make them take their chance.

---

52   **yelled** [jeld] : shouted.

"Daughters draw with their husbands' families, Tessie," Mr Summers
225 said gently. "You know that as well as anyone else."

"It wasn't *fair*!" Tessie said.

"I guess not, Joe," Bill Hutchinson said regretfully. [53] "My daughter
draws with her husband's family, that's only fair. And I've got no other
family except the kids.

230 "Then, as far as drawing for families is concerned, it's you," Mr
Summers said explanation, "and as far as drawing for households is
concerned that's you, too. Right?"

"Right," Bill Hutchinson said.

"How many kids, Bill?" Mr Summers asked formally.

235 "Three," Bill Hutchinson said. "There's Bill, Jr., and Nancy, and little
Daye. And Tessie and me."

"All right, then," Mr Summers said. "Harry, you got their tickets
back?"

Mr Graves nodded and held up the slips of paper. "Put them in the
240 box, then," Mr Summers directed. "Take Bill's and put it in."

"I think we ought to start over," Mrs Hutchinson said, as quietly as
she could. "I tell you it wasn't *fair*. You didn't give him time enough to
choose. Everybody saw that."

Mr Graves had selected the five slips and put them in the box, and he
245 dropped all the papers [54] but those onto the ground, where the breeze
caught them and lifted them off.

"Listen, everybody," Mrs Hutchinson was saying to the people
around her.

"Ready, Bill?" Mr Summers asked, and Bill Hutchinson, with one
250 quick glance around at his wife and children, nodded.

"Remember," Mr Summers said, "take the slips and keep them folded
until each person has taken one. Harry, you help little Dave." Mr Graves
took the hand of the little boy, who came willingly with him up to the
box. "Take a paper out of the box, Davy," Mr Summers said. Davy put his
255 hand into the box and laughed. "Take just *one* paper," Mr Summers said.

---

53   **regretfully** : sadly.

54   **dropped all the papers** : let the papers fall to the ground.

"Harry, you hold it for him." Mr Graves took the child's hand and removed·the folded paper from the right fist and held it while little Dave stood next to him and looked up at him wonderingly. [55]

"Nancy next," Mr Summers said. Nancy was twelve, and her school friends breathed heavily, as she went forward, switching [56] her skirt, and took a slip daintily [57] from the box. "Bill Jr.," Mr Summers said, and Billy, his face red and his feet overlarge, nearly knocked the box over as he got a paper out. "Tessie," Mr Summers said. She hesitated for a minute, looking around defiantly, [58] and then set lips and went up to the box. She snatched [59] a paper out and held it behind her.

260

265

"Bill," Mr Summers said, and Bill Hutchinson reached into the box and felt around, bringing his hand out at last with the slip of paper in it.

The crowd was quiet. A girl whispered, "I hope it's not Nancy," and the sound of the whisper reached the edges [60] of the crowd.

  a Who has picked the "winning" ticket?

....

  b Is everyone happy about the result of the lottery?

....

  c How can you account for Tessie's "It wasn't *fair*'?

....

55   **wonderingly** ['wʌndərɪŋli] : without understanding.

56   **switching** : swinging.

57   **daintily** : gracefully.

58   **defiantly** [dɪ'faɪəntli] : boldly.

59   **snatched** : took quickly.

60   **edges** ['edʒɪz] : (here) periphery.

d Who are Don and Eva?

....

e Why can't they be included in the final draw?

....

f How many people take part in the final draw?

....

g What does the girl's whisper "I hope it is not Nancy" add to your understanding of the story?

....

12 Now that you have read more of the story, go back to Activity 8 and rediscuss it. Are your views still the same?

13 How do you think the story will end? Now read the final part of the story.

270   "It's not the way it used to be," Old Man Warner said clearly. "People ain't the way they used to be."

"All right," Mr Summers said. "Open the papers. Harry, you open little Dave's."

Mr Graves opened the slip of paper, and there was a general sigh
275   through the crowd as he held it up and everyone could see that it was blank. 61 Nancy and Bill Jr., opened theirs at the same time, and both beamed 62 and laughed, turning around to the crowd and holding their slips above their heads.

"Tessie," Mr Summers said. There was a pause, and then Mr Summers
280   looked at Bill Hutchinson, and Bill unfolded his paper and showed it. It was blank.

61   **blank** : not written on.
62   **beamed** [biːmd] : smiled radiantly.

"It's Tessie," Mr Summers said, and his voice was hushed. [63] "Show us her paper, Bill."

Bill Hutchinson went over to his wife and forced the slip of paper out of the hand. It had a black spot on it, the black spot Mr Summers had   285
made the night before with the heavy pencil in the coal-company office. Bill Hutchinson held it up, and there was a stir in the crowd.

"All right, folks," Mr Summers said, "Let's finish quickly."

Although the villagers had forgotten the ritual and lost the original black box, they still remembered to use stones. The pile of stones the boys   290
had made earlier was ready; there were stones on the ground with the blowing [64] scraps [65] of paper that had come out of the box. Mrs Delacroix selected a stone so large she had to pick it up with both hands and turned to Mrs Dunbar. "Come on," she said. "Hurry up."

Mrs Dunbar had small stones in both hands, and she said, gasping for   295
breath, "I can't run at all. You'll have to go ahead and I'll catch up with you."

The children had stones already, and someone gave little Davy Hutchinson a few pebbles.

Tessie Hutchinson was in the center of a cleared [66] space by now, and   300
she held her hands out desperately as the villagers moved in on her. "It isn't fair," she said. A stone hit her on the side of the head.

Old Man Warner saying, "Come on, come on, everyone." Steve Adams was in the front of the crowd of villagers, with Mrs Graves beside him.

"It isn't fair, it isn't right," Mrs Hutchinson screamed, [67] and then they   305
were upon her.

---

63   **hushed** [hʌʃt] : silenced.

64   **blowing** ['bləʊɪŋ] : moving because of the wind.

65   **scraps** : small pieces, fragments.

66   **cleared** ['klɪəd] : empty.

67   **screamed** : cried loudly in fear.

14 Were your predictions about the ending right or wrong? If they were right, say which clues in the text helped you to come to the right conclusions. If they were wrong, what methods does the narrator use to "trick" the reader?

Now reconsider the story as a whole.

15 What are the prevailing themes in this story? Look at the list of possibilities given below, select up to four words you consider appropriate (you may also add your own) and rate them on the scale according to their relevance to the story.

- individualism   • solidarity   • indifference   • cynicism
- the instinct for survival   • cruelty   • other

+   −

16 How would you define "The Lottery"?

- a realistic portrait of man's most basic instincts
- human sacrifice and propitiatory ritual
- a story of ignorance and superstition
- a fantastic story about an unlikely situation
- an allegory about the dark side of human nature
- a story about a sect of racist fanatics
- a macabre account of obsolete practices
- other

17 a Focus on language and style. Read the alternatives given below and say which one(s) you agree with. Find evidence in the text to support your choice.

- There is cohesion at lexical level created mainly through repetition of words (adjectives, nouns, adverbs, definite article).

- Through the use of adverbs the reader is made aware that the narrator is judging the characters and their actions.

- Sentences are long in the description and report modes.

- The language is subtle and formal throughout the text.

- Dialogue is generally concise and to the point.

- The dialogue contains examples of ellipsis, non-standard words and Americanisms.

b In general how would you define the style? Choose from the following words or add your own. Back up your answer with examples from the text.

- objective   • literary   • figurative   • colloquial

- concise   • descriptive   • elaborate   • emotional

c Is the language used appropriate to the subject matter?

18 The story opens with a description of the setting. Do you feel that this description is detailed enough to give you a clear picture of the setting? What does the way in which the setting is described add to our understanding of the story? Go through the list of possibilities given below and tick the one(s) you agree with (or add your own).

- The reader is given no more than an outline of the setting. This lack of contextualization places the story outside any easily identifiable period of time and makes it more universal.

- The setting is described in great detail, it represents the externalization of the mood and feelings of the people.

- The setting is in sharp contrast to the situation and makes the ending more unexpected.

- Other

19 Where do you think the author's main interests lie?

- in the development of characters and their psychology
- in conveying an idea, or a particular point of view
- in shocking the reader
- in providing a sort of criticism
- in creating suspense and tension
- other

20 Discuss your reaction to the story. Does the story contain any optimistic elements?

Beyond the text

Talking points

1 Although initially shocking, "The Lottery" is in fact much closer to reality than it might seem at first glance.
There are often articles in the newspapers or news items on the television about fanatic religious sects carrying out collective killings or mass suicides. Human sacrifice is as old as man. Discuss.

2 "The Midas Catch. Oh, the pleasure in those unlucky lottery numbers!"
In Great Britain the National Lottery is a recent institution (December '95), welcomed by most of the population. The press has often dealt with the topic, sometimes reporting about winners who said that they in fact regretted winning such huge amounts of money.
Read the article below. What is it about?
Choose from the suggestions given below (or add your own):

- a man who won the lottery and became extraordinarily rich and extraordinarily unhappy
- people's obsession with money
- people's attitude to lotteries
- people's reaction to other people's "good luck"

THE MIDAS CATCH
Oh, the pleasure in those unlucky lottery numbers!

To scoop [1] the lottery jackpot is the modern version of winning the Derby, marrying a millionaire and finding a crock of gold [2] at the end of the rainbow. It is the weekly dream that might transform your life, and actually does transform somebody else's.

Last week's winner woke up to find himself richer by £22.5 million. But the concomitant nightmare to his dream is that he has been hounded into hiding with his name splashed over the newspapers in less than complimentary terms. His wife described him as a cheating rat and declared: "I'll screw him for every penny he's got." His adoptive mother found harsher words, and added that she hoped he drank himself to death.

This is not the first time that the lottery has brought bad as well as good luck. The winner of the first roll-over jackpot in December has had to change his name and become a recluse in his palatian [3] new home. With riches, the lottery has brought family feuds, divorce and public abuse, as well as suicide.

There is also something in human nature that enjoys this misfortune in the fortune of others. If somebody runs after money, he is labelled money-mad; if he keeps it, he is a Scrooge; [4] if he spends it, he is a waster. If he does not try to get money, he has no ambition; if he gets it without working, he is a parasite; and if he accumulates it after a lifetime of hard work, people call him an old fogey [5] who has never got anything out of life.

To judge from our infatuation with the lottery, most of us would like to be millionaires.

Money cannot buy you love, though it does put you in a better bargaining position. Money cannot buy you health, though it will pay for your BUPA [6] subscription, a private hospital, and a grand funeral. Money cannot buy you happiness, but it will provide on tap the best therapists, public relations officers and lawyers that money can buy. So the misfortunes of the latest lottery-winner have sent a shiver of malicious pleasure through the nation. But they will not stop our nation of punters [7] wagering millions on unlucky numbers next Saturday.

(from THE TIMES)

What is the overall tone of this article? Is the last paragraph saying something different from the rest of the article?

1 **scoop** : get something, esp. a large amount of money.

2 **crock of gold** : a pot of gold (supposed to be found at the end of the rainbow).

3 **palatian** : resembling a palace.

4 **Scrooge** [skru:dʒ] : (infml derog.) very ingenerous person.

5 **fogey** ['fəʊgi] : person who dislikes change and has old-fashioned ideas.

6 **BUPA** : a well-known private health insurance company.

7 **punters** : (infml) gamblers.

BIBLIOGRAPHY

CARTER, R. and LONG, M., *Teaching Literature*, Longman, 1991.

CARTER, R. and LONG, M., *The Web of Words*, Cambridge University Press, 1987.

CHATMAN, S., *Story and Discourse*, Cornell University Press, 1991.

COLLIE, JOANNE and SLATER, STEPHEN, *Literature in the Language Classroom*, Cambridge University Press, 1987.

CUDDON, J. A., *Dictionary of Literary Terms and Literary Theory*, Penguin, 1991.

GROSSER, H., *Narrativa*, Principato, 1985.

LEECH, G. N., and SHORT, M. H., *Style in Fiction*, Longman, 1981.

MARCHESE, A., *Dizionario di retorica e di stilistica*, Arnoldo Mondadori, 1978.

REID, J., *The Short Story*, Methuen, 1977.

SHAW, V., *The Short Story: A Critical Introduction*, Longman, 1983.

WIDDOWSON, H. G., *Stylistic and the Teaching of Literature*, Longman, 1975.